Graham Taylor, Hartford Theological Seminary

A Memorial of the semi-centenary Celebration of the founding

of the Theological Institute of Connecticut

Graham Taylor, Hartford Theological Seminary

A Memorial of the semi-centenary Celebration of the founding
of the Theological Institute of Connecticut

ISBN/EAN: 9783337076238

Printed in Europe, USA, Canada, Australia, Japan

Cover: Foto ©ninafisch / pixelio.de

More available books at **www.hansebooks.com**

A MEMORIAL

OF THE

SEMI-CENTENARY CELEBRATION

OF THE

FOUNDING

OF THE

THEOLOGICAL INSTITUTE

OF CONNECTICUT.

PREFATORY NOTE.

At the annual meeting of the Pastoral Union of Connecticut, in the Chapel of Hosmer Hall, Hartford, May 8, 1884, Rev. Graham Taylor, Rev. John H. Goodell, and J. M. Allen, Esq., were appointed a committee to publish at their discretion the proceedings of the semi-centennial celebration of the Theological Institute of Connecticut.

Congratulating the officers and students, the graduates and friends of the Institute upon the record of its past history, the substantial and invaluable attainments of the present, and the still brighter prospects of growing power and usefulness in the future, the Committee present as a fitting Memorial of the Semi-Centennial Anniversary,

I. A brief account of the observance of the occasion.

II. The papers, addresses, and letters prepared for the celebration *abridged* in accordance with the design of this publication.

III. An appendix containing reports of the past year's work, an account of the closing exercises with the address of Professor Riddle to the Graduating Class.

THE SEMI-CENTENNIAL ANNIVERSARY.

In May 1883, a committee representing the Pastoral Union, Trustees, Faculty, and Alumni, was appointed to make arrangements for the celebration of the semi-centennial anniversary of the Institute. At an early day, all who had been students of the Seminary, and the members of the Pastoral Union, received a cordial invitation to participate in the memorial observance on Wednesday, May 7, 1884. Special invitations were also extended to many residents of Hartford, and notices of the services were published in the local newspapers.

Returning alumni and invited guests were welcomed to the generous hospitality of the homes of the many friends of the Seminary in the city.

From a wider extent of territory than was ever before represented on any occasion in the history of the Institute, its graduates and friends gathered in numbers that did honor to the commemoration, and betokened their loyalty to its past and future.

Assurances of warm interest in the Institution and its jubilee were received from foreign and home missionaries and pastors, unable to be present.

The weather all through the anniversary days was unpropitious. A cold northeast storm prevailed; but the attendance at the business meeting of the Alumni Association, at an early hour on Wednesday, was large. Rev. Dr. A. C. Thompson was chosen president, Rev. S. B. Forbes of Rockville, Conn., vice-president, with Rev. G. W. Winch of Enfield, secretary for three years. Appropriate mention was made of the death of Rev. M. S. Goodale, D.D., of Amsterdam, N. Y., of the class of '36, the first that graduated from the Seminary, and who was to have given a paper on Dr. Nettleton on this occasion, also of Rev. Benjamin Howe, class of '41, of Linebrook, Ipswich, Mass.

The Chapel of Hosmer Hall, and one of the adjoining rooms, were filled at the opening of the commemorative exercises, by the large audience, which, besides the guests from abroad, included many friends from the city.

At ten o'clock Rev. S. B. Forbes, vice-president of the Alumni Association, took the chair, and called upon Rev. Dr. Laurie of Providence, to offer prayer. Rev. Lyman Whiting, D.D., read the Scriptures, and after singing, Mr. Rowland Swift, in behalf of the Trustees and the citizens of Hartford, delivered a most felicitous and hearty address of welcome.

Rev. Professor William Thompson, the venerable Dean of the Faculty, then delivered the Historical Discourse, reviewing, as only an eye-witness could, the life and work of the Institute during the half-century of its existence, and of his own life-work in its service.

Rev. Lavalette Perrin, D.D., followed with a paper on Dr. Bennet Tyler, the Seminary's only "President" and first Professor of Theology.

The close and vital "Relation of the Seminary to the Cause of Foreign Missions," was thoroughly and interestingly developed by Rev. Dr. A. C. Thompson of Boston.

The hour for recess having arrived, it was necessary to omit the reading of Rev. Dr. H. M. Parsons' tribute to the ever-blessed memory of Rev. Asahel Nettleton, D.D., whose character and work are sacredly cherished among the successive generations of students as a most precious inheritance of the past, and a bright goal of their high calling.

The intermission afforded a pleasant opportunity for the social reunion and intercourse of the large company present. The main hall and its adjoining rooms were thronged with ladies and gentlemen, many of the latter meeting, after long separation, as old friends and fellow-students.

At 1 o'clock two hundred and fifty guests were seated in

the music room, and two adjoining class-rooms, where an ample collation was handsomely served, after the blessing had been asked by President Noah Porter of Yale College.

To the Chairman of the Prudential Committee, Mr. George Kellogg, and the many ladies who so kindly assisted his efforts, all were indebted for the very thoughtful and complete provision for their comfort and enjoyment.

The chapel was again well filled by those who reassembled to enjoy the exercises of the afternoon, which were happily conducted by Professor Lewellyn Pratt, in place of Rev. Dr. Henry M. Field, who had accepted the invitation to preside, but was unable to be present.

The paper presented by Rev. John H. Goodell of Windsor Locks, on "The Biblical Teaching of the Seminary—its Distinctive Feature," was listened to with marked interest as a contribution of permanent value to the Institution.

From a large number of letters received by the committee from the alumni and other friends, Rev. W. S. Hawkes of South Hadley Falls, Mass., read carefully selected and copious extracts, which were heard with evident pleasure by all, and with personal interest by many. These reminiscences presented a varied and graphic picture of the successive periods of seminary life, as seen from within, which will be treasured in printed form by many more than those who heard their recital.

"Several carefully prepared impromptu addresses" were then announced by the chairman.

The first to respond was Rev. Dr. Cushing Eells of the class of '37, who told the thrilling story of his missionary life and labors in Oregon and Washington Territories during the past forty-five years of service. In his allusion to his intimate relation with the martyred Dr. Whitman, in the early history of the great Northwest, he became truly "the old man eloquent." Upon his retirement, the fact was related that while thus engaged in missionary work amid the hardships of frontier life, he and his wife had earned and given to the cause of Christian education over fifteen thousand dollars.

Rev. Francis Williams of the class of '41, spoke facetiously of the social life at East Windsor Hill when he was a student there.

President Porter of Yale presented the salutations of that sister seminary, with many bright and interesting allusions to the past and present relations between the two institutions.

Rev. Graham Taylor of Hartford, referred to the indebtedness of the city pastors for the library privileges so freely granted them at Hosmer Hall. He alluded to the deep obligation felt by many of the city churches for the valuable assistance rendered by the students in their Sunday-schools and prayer-meetings. The appreciation of their presence and services by people and pastors is very apparent each year, in the many ways in which, he assured them, their absence is felt. On behalf of the "Pastors' Mission," he thanked the students, especially for the noble response they had made to the appeal for their aid in conducting evangelistic services in the most destitute parts of the city. Nearly all of them had volunteered service. The unfailing regularity with which they had met their appointments, and the spirit and efficiency with which they had done "the work of an evangelist," not only in the services, but in thoroughly canvassing whole sections of the city, and in calling as opportunity invited from house to house, deserved a public recognition as hearty as the personal appreciation it had received from all directly associated with them in the work.

The varied programme of the afternoon was brought to a close by the reading of a poem entitled "The Survival of the Axe," prepared for the occasion by Rev. Theron Brown, of the class of 1859, a Baptist clergyman of Norwood, Mass. The play of its feeling, humorous and earnest, met with appreciative response from his amused and interested auditors.

The commemorative services of the day were fittingly closed with the concert of the "Hosmer Hall Choral Union," in the Asylum Hill Congregational Church, in the evening, under the direction of Associate-Professor Waldo S. Pratt, with a chorus numbering one hundred and seventy-five voices, including almost all the seminary students, and with the assistance of soloists and orchestra from abroad, the Union rendered Handel's Oratorio, "The Messiah."

The audience completely filled the spacious edifice, and included the alumni and guests of the Seminary, to all whom complimentary admission was tendered by the generosity of the Trustees. The public indebtedness to the Seminary for the eminent character of the performance was well expressed in the following hearty recognition by the Hartford "Courant":

"It is so long since the Messiah was given in this city that the public owes a debt to the Choral Union for giving it, and a double debt for giving it so well as was done last evening. Some of the obligation must extend over to the Theological Seminary, since it is largely through it that the performance became possible. It not only furnishes a considerable share of the singers, but has given place for rehearsal, furnished the director, and done very much more, directly and indirectly, towards developing and strengthening the Union. Without the Seminary it would hardly have come into existence, and certainly would not have had so good an opportunity for development into an enthusiastic society with a high aim and a better conception of the purpose of music of the highest order than has yet existed here. Each of the performances given since the initial one has shown a marked advance, and this last was no exception to the established rule.

"When from a body chosen mainly out of those who have an enthusiasm for study and practice, such admirable results can come, as were produced last evening, it evidences very remarkable ability on the part of the instructor. Those who have often heard the Messiah, and compare the rendering of the choruses last evening with those of the Handel and Haydn Society of Boston, the Sacred Harmonic Society of London, and similar organizations, must confess that while, of course, weak in the grand effects, there was not simply a precision, a technical mastery of difficulties, but better still, an intelligence of comprehension and a poetry of execution which are almost never surpassed. It was not simple earnestness, but there was a delicacy of shading, a studious force of contrasts, a breadth of style which showed the most careful study of the piece, viewed as a great religious work. In a word, it was given in a manner quite in keeping with the Institution under whose auspices it was performed. These qualities were so uniformly displayed that it is not necessary to select instances. Of course, with a chorus of less than two hundred, with a small orchestra, and an organ not of first magnitude, the thrilling effects produced by numbers cannot be gained; but it may be said that the 'Hallelujah' and the closing chorus, 'Worthy is the Lamb,' were a surprise to all in their massive and stirring power. But all had been equally studied, and revealed in the details the supervision of a skilled director, and the most painstaking practice. The impression made upon the crowded audience was one of surprise, pleasure, and satisfaction."

The annual devotional service, held on Thursday morning, was more largely attended than usual, and most appropriately conducted by Rev. H. C. Alvord. Brethren widely sundered for years found the hour of spiritual fellowship most delightful and refreshing.

The afternoon was devoted to the annual meeting of the Pastoral Union, whose business proceedings, reported in the Appendix, were enlivened by a thrilling address of congratulation and sympathy, by Rev. Dr. E. B. Webb of Boston, who succeeded this year to the Presidency of the Board of Trustees.

The closing exercises in the evening were very largely attended. Rev. Dr. A. J. F. Behrends of Brooklyn, delivered the last lecture in the Carew course on "The Relation of the Mind of Man to the Revelation of God." His profoundly philosophical treatment of the theme was designed to demonstrate the capacity of man's mind to receive, respond to, and interpret the revealed thought of God.

The memorable series of services was concluded by the eminently appropriate and practical address of Rev. Professor Riddle to the graduating class, which is the fitting conclusion to this Memorial volume.

ADDRESSES AND LETTERS.

Address of Welcome.

BY ROWLAND SWIFT, ESQ.

Mr. President, Alumni, and friends:

As one looks about him here, just now, there is something in the very motion and composure of this gathered company that is suggestive of the season of reunion and repast for kindred hearts. I am sure that something of the old-time spirit of the Pilgrims' Jubilee, grave indeed, but fervid too and even exuberant, is abroad in the assembly and moving upon the surface and through the depths of it.

A narrative of early colonial times tells of the reward to public and united prayers, when the rains saved the shriveling crops: "Having these many signs of God's favor and acception we thought it would be great ingratitude if, secretly, we should smother up the same or content ourselves with private thanksgiving for that which by private prayer could not be obtained." Cotton Mather recorded the information that Mr. Eliot taught his Indian converts "to set apart their days for both fasting and prayer and for feasting and prayer," and that they, the devout Indians, "performed the duties of those days with a very laborious piety." I hope we shall do as well as they, with less fatigue and possibly as appropriately; but it is our turn to-day to celebrate; it is our calling to rejoice and give thanks, not secretly, at the manifold things of divine bestowal which we have received.

The committee have honored me with a request that I should say a few words for them at this stage of your proceedings. I wish, at the same time, that what I have to offer, so very briefly as will be necessary, may be commended to your acceptance as the hearty greeting of a citizen of Hartford, for I cannot avoid associating, in a manner, events which we celebrate in this presence, with others inevitably to be recalled to mind as we go on, and which are happily so much in harmony with this occasion. I assume, as a fact, that this memorial service to which you have been invited, commemorates one of the accomplishments which is fairly illustrative of the old-time character of our Christian citizenship—its loyalty, its wisdom, and its piety.

I presume you will not forget that probably before ever a kernel of wheat was sown upon these hills or even a furrow had been traced across the virgin intervals, our provident forefathers had hewed and planted and covered in the beams of their little sanctuary. The colony was still very young when Hopkins, first the merchant citizen, then the chief magistrate, had set apart a significant portion of his estate by will, "to give some encouragement for the breeding up of hopeful youths both at the grammar school and college, for the public service of the country in future times," supplementing this first provision by another, as he so positively set forth, "in further prosecution of the aforesaid public ends, which, in the simplicity of my heart, are for the upholding and promoting the Kingdom of the Lord Jesus Christ in those parts of the earth."

It is assuring to remind ourselves how the land was possessed, and how orderly and characteristic was the progress of Christian enterprise. A city that began, well back in the last century, to gather its public libraries, and to multiply its churches; where, from common school to college, seminaries of learning have increased as rapidly as riches; where, in due time, were planted homes for the orphan, retreat for the insane, asylum and training-school for the deaf and dumb, reformatories for the inebriate, hospitals for the sick and injured, houses of refuge for the aged and infirm, and numerous other distinctively Christian enterprises, to this day doing their beneficent and sacred work—Hartford, at the appointed time, not lacking a citizenship equal to the opportunity, after thoughtful observation and deliberation, of course adopted this consecrated school. It was like Hartford to do it; to do it in a way that should bring to record that measured decision that goes with purpose and faith; and if you would see a chart of the willing mind that is accepted according to what a man hath and not according to what he hath not, look over, some day, the lists of saintly donors enrolled upon the old subscription books. She who cast in of her living has written her name there, and the well-to-do men of the time have honored the page and their names and their city by varying and increasing and noble gifts.

Here the renovated institution was not out of place. New associations were and are felicitous, and you who, to-day, return here for the first time, find yourselves here at home, and we together, citizens and alumni, may reverently give thanks for what we see not only within these walls, but for the legacy of unnumbered names ever to be remembered with Hopkins's and Wadsworth's and Watkinson's and Gallaudet's and Hosmer's, because of their co-operation in those beneficent projects which best adorn our neighboring landscapes, and most significantly characterize our civilization.

With the close of our half century we would gladly have welcomed full numbers to our golden festival. A timely summons, as hopefully importunate as could be framed, went abroad to every name upon your rolls of survivors. Many are marked "not present" this morning, yet it will seem so often, while you are together, as if they were very near and verily of your company!

I have been told that on the shores of the Adriatic, there may be heard, at nightfall of almost any day, the sweet snatches of song that are sent out by waiting mothers and children who expect, through the deepening shadows, the return of husband or brother. From afar out upon the waters, responding strains are heard at last, and though distant and but faintly to be heard, how do they reward and animate the heart of loving wife and child! They sing to and fro from beach to boat as the tired but blessed fishermen are guided to their rock and to their home!

In the mountains of the Tyrol, too, they say such another call rises, at the cottage-doors of the shepherds, from those who love them and who come out at sunset and listen, sometimes long, for the answering music that shall tell them that, from the pastures where they find verdure and danger, the herdsman, though belated, is coming homeward with all his flock. The song that flies from cot to cliff, and from cliff to cot, ceases never until man and herd are brought safely to home and rest. In such expressive sympathy will you find yourselves with your absent brethren, when in due course you hear from them by and bye. Our overtures that were sent across the seas brought responses that thrill the heart like a heroic song. They seem to say: "We have cast our net on the other side of the ship. We shall find. The master said so. It is filling; we cannot leave it till we bring it safe, unbroken to the land!"

From the mountains of the west others sent answers of regret, but so praiseful that their cheer comes very close home. "Thank God for our ninety-and-nine. We seek those that remain, that have been given to us; when they are found —it will not be long—we will come home; then, friends, we will have rest, and rejoice together." But I am not unmindful how the time speeds on to-day. The fervent grip of your hands with one another has already had its spell, and the irrepressible interchange of news and assurance, a longer charm. So the Anniversary will quickly weave its shining golden thread across and through the texture of the onward extending life.

God bless you, friends, and give you cheer when you must go again from the restful holiday to the waiting field, but a brimful, New England Thanksgiving welcome to you while you stay!

Historical Address.

BY PROFESSOR WILLIAM THOMPSON.

To some who favor us with their presence this morning, the establishment and early fortunes of the Theological Institute of Connecticut are a familiar story. They were old enough in 1834 to read and hear what was said, and done by its advocates and opponents. They have not been indifferent observers of its ongoings from one decade to another. But of the men who started the enterprise, and of its singular experiences, few of you retain from personal knowledge a clear impression. The survey now proposed is chiefly for a younger class of hearers, more or less curious to learn how the Seminary fared while it remained at East Windsor Hill.

"New England Theology" is an ambiguous phrase. The varieties of belief denoted by this term at different periods have always been spoken of with special reference to Congregationalists. Before the time of Pres. Edwards, New England divines held the Calvinistic views embodied substantially in Willard's Lectures on the Assembly's Catechism. Whatever modifications of theological belief were afterwards adopted, the system remained essentially the same, and it has long been customary to name as its chief expounders and advocates in the last century Edwards, Bellamy, and Dwight. Its more recent representatives in New England were Woods and Tyler. The views held by these writers differ but little from those embodied in the creeds of New England churches from the earliest period in their history to a very recent day. They are sometimes designated as "Old Calvinism," sometimes "Old School Theology."

The tenets set forth by a class of theologians claiming to be "consistent Calvinists," led by Drs. Emmons and Hopkins, have been styled in some quarters "New England Theology." But what these eminent divines taught as "improvements" on the doctrinal system long accepted among us never gained a currency sufficiently wide to justify this title.

More recently the speculations of Dr. Nathaniel W. Taylor and his associates have been known to a moderate extent by the same name. They are more properly known as the "New Divinity of New England," or "New Haven Divinity." In the year 1822 the Theological Department of Yale College was organized in its present form, and Dr. Nathaniel W. Taylor was appointed professor. The founder of his professorship required that as a condition of holding office the incumbent should give his assent to the Saybrook Platform, the doctrinal part of which instrument is in full accord with the Assembly's Catechism. It was the accredited formula of a large proportion of the Congregational churches in New England.

Not long after the inauguration of Dr. Taylor it became known to some of his intimate ministerial friends, of whom Dr. Nettleton was one, that he held theories and speculations not in agreement with the acknowledged standards of orthodoxy. In his *Concio ad Clerum*, preached Sept. 10, 1828, sentiments and hypotheses were avowed which awakened widespread anxiety. Two years before this Prof. Fitch preached a sermon on "Sin," which was generally considered as antagonistic to evangelical doctrine. Various attempts were made to prevent open controversy, but they proved futile. Personal expostulation, correspondence, conferences of representative men, all failed to quiet the rising agitation or restrain the New Haven divines from advocating their sentiments through the press.

The tenets of Dr. Taylor which created disquietude, it is believed, may be fairly stated as follows:

First. God could not have prevented all sin in a moral system.

Second. Mankind came into the world with the same nature in kind as that with which Adam was created, and the fact that his posterity uniformly sin is due to the circumstances in which they are placed.

Third. Self-love is the primary cause of all moral action. The exact form of the thesis was in these words: "Of all specific voluntary action the happiness of the agent, in some form, is the ultimate end."

Fourth. Antecedent to regeneration the selfish principle is suspended in the sinner's heart, so that he ceases to sin and uses the means of regeneration with motives that are neither sinful nor holy.

In the leading religious quarterly of New England at that time, the *Christian Spectator*, these dogmas were set forth with great earnestness, eloquence, and skill by eminent divines, who shared the prestige of our chief literary institution, and of the general respect and confidence won by their eminent attainments and services. To protest publicly against the sentiments avowed by such writers, holding exalted positions and assured of powerful support, was a step from which ministers of the gospel and intelligent laymen naturally recoiled. But there seemed to be no option. Individual remonstrances and entreaties had failed to prevent the wide dissemination of theological sentiments believed by many to be fraught with incalculable mischief. This apprehension of danger was deeply felt by Jeremiah Evarts, Gov. John Cotton Smith, Drs. Tyler, Nettleton, Humphrey, Griffin, Ebenezer Porter, Woods, and other leading men in New England and in various quarters. If any persons were competent to estimate correctly the difference between the New Haven Theology and what the Congregational churches and ministers of New England generally and firmly believed to be the teachings of the Divine Word, they were found among those who struck the first note of alarm. The more thoroughly the New Haven Divinity was examined, the more clearly it appeared to be antagonistic to biblical views of the divine government, human depravity, regeneration, and the essential difference between the motives that govern renewed and unrenewed men. Perhaps the time has not yet come for an impartial judgment on the merits of the controversy and the spirit in which it was conducted. With some confidence, however, an unbiased inquirer may be referred to what was written at the most exciting stage of the discussion by Drs. Dow, Nettleton, Tyler, and Woods, as seldom marred by asperity or unfairness. Such a reader would not fail of seeing that these men were profoundly moved in view of doctrinal innovations imperiling the purity of revivals and the spiritual vigor of the churches.

No branch of the new divinity awakened more general fear and regret than what was currently styled at the time " Regeneration by self-love." Near the fatal close of his long illness Dr. Nettleton was visited by his old ministerial friend, the acknowledged leader of the new movement, with whose views he had been sorely grieved. Shortly after the interview he wrote to his distinguished visitor, concluding his letter as follows: " I would cherish the hope that your own religious experience is at variance with some things which you have published; particularly on the subject of self-love, and the great doctrine of regeneration. It does seem to me I experienced all which you make essential to regeneration, while, as I now fully believe, my heart was unreconciled to God. And this is the reason that leads me to fear that what you have written will be the means of deceiving and destroying souls. I say this with the kindest feelings and with eternity in view. Receive it as my dying testimony and as an expression of my sincere love."

With such positive convictions respecting the views persistently advocated in high places as " great improvements " on the old theology thirty-six Connecticut Congregational ministers met in convention at East (now South) Windsor, Sept. 10, 1833, " for the purpose of consultation and taking such measures as may be deemed expedient for the defense and promotion of evangelical principles." The sessions were held in a small ancient brick school-house about half a mile north of the present Congregational church. The more prominent members of the body were Drs. Samuel Spring, Asahel Nettleton, Nathaniel Hewitt, Daniel Dow, G. A. Calhoun,

Joseph Harvey, and Rev. Cyrus Yale. Only three of the thirty-six delegates are now living. The two days in that secluded brick school-house devoted to prayerful deliberation were marked by the absence of party-spirit and unmistakable tokens of the divine presence. The result was the organization of the Conn. Pastoral Union, and shortly after the Theological Institute of Connecticut. At a session of the Legislature in the ensuing spring an act of incorporation was obtained, allowing the trustees to hold property to the amount of fifty thousand dollars. Upon the petition of the trustees in 1859 the charter was so amended that the Institute could hold any real or personal estate, provided the annual income thereof should not exceed twelve thousand dollars.

The location of the Seminary at East Windsor was chiefly due to the generous aid proffered by Mr. Erastus Ellsworth, who had recently retired to that town after a prosperous business career in New York. If other friends have made larger donations to the Institute, no one is better entitled to be called its foster-father. In its early days of weakness and subsequent perils Erastus Ellsworth promptly responded to every call that taxed his purse, time, patience, or capacity as a man of affairs. On the 13th of May, 1834, the cornerstone of the seminary edifice was laid by the venerable Dr. Perkins of West Hartford, and two professors were inducted into office: Dr. Bennett Tyler, Professor of Theology, and Dr. Jonathan Cogswell, Professor of Sacred History. During the previous winter fifteen students had received instruction from Dr. Tyler. On the 14th of the following October the Professor of Biblical Literature entered on his duties. The regular course of instruction now began, sixteen students being in attendance. Two stories of the seminary building were ready for use, and about two thousand volumes, chiefly given by Connecticut pastors, had been placed on the shelves of the library.

In their first report to the Pastoral Union the trustees advert to the " prayerful solicitude and trembling hope " with which the resolution was adopted " under an imperious sense of duty to the Great Head of the Church and implicit reliance upon his blessing, to proceed to the establishment of a new seminary for the education of young men for the gospel ministry." With limited means and under great discouragements the guardians of the young enterprise found their first year's experience fitted to " excite their gratitude and animate their hopes." "The increasing confidence and favor of the Christian public" was noted with special gratification. The whole amount of subscriptions to May 1st, 1835, was thirty-three thousand seven hundred thirty-three dollars. The largest donation was that of $1,250 from Mr. David N. Lord of the city of New York. A large proportion of the gifts by which the current expenses of the Institute were met during its first years was in small sums by persons of moderate means. For a time the trustees judged that when the cost of buildings had been defrayed an income of $3,000 annually would be sufficient, and that it would be better to obtain this sum by yearly subscriptions than to aim at permanent endowments.

Could any one expect that the establishment of a second theological seminary in Connecticut would escape hostile criticism? In the fall of 1834 the theological Professors of Yale College published a statement denying that any good reason could be assigned for the new enterprise. This called out an "Appeal to the Public in behalf of the Institute." The trustees defended their action on the ground that the theological school at New Haven was under the entire control of a corporation, nearly one-half of whose members are such men as one political party or another happens to choose for State officers. By a change in recent years the alumni choose six members of the corporation. It is not apparent that this measure increases the security of the Theological Department. Reference was also made by our trustees to the feeling of insecurity awakened among the churches by the disclosure of the fact that three of the Professors in the New Haven Seminary were not required to give their assent to any confession of faith. The Professor of Theology was indeed bound to declare "his free assent to the Confession of Faith and Ecclesiastical Discipline agreed upon by the Churches of this State in the year 1708." This refers to the Saybrook Platform, which in doctrine is identical with the Assembly's Catechism. But, to the surprise of the public, it was now announced that Dr. Taylor "had certain knowledge, from personal intercourse with the founders (of his professorship), that if he had embraced every minute doctrine of the Confession it would have been considered a decisive disqualification for the office." Consequently it was claimed that, while the Professor of Theology held and taught doctrines at variance with the creed, he could not be impeached, because his assent had been given only for substance of doctrine.

A still more weighty reason for their action was assigned by our trustees. It was the deep and wide-spread dissatisfaction produced by the publication and defense of the New Haven views. These have been already stated.

A subordinate motive for organizing a new seminary was the growing demand for more adequate physical exercise by candidates for the sacred office. Extended investigations had lately shown that an alarming percentage, fully one-half, of those who deserve the character of close students, injured themselves by neglect of bodily exercise. An early grave or chronic weakness and disease were the penalty to be expected in the case of many promising aspirants for the ministry. To check this fearful loss of consecrated talent it was resolved to provide ample means for manual labor in the new school of the prophets.

The prejudices of many good people were roused against the Institute by the persistent accusation that it was divisive in its aims and spirit, and foretokened the breaking up of existing ecclesiastical relations in this state. The answer was that no such purpose was entertained. It was said: "While we concede to our brethren who differ from us the right to think for themselves and to inculcate their own opinions, we ask them to allow us the same privilege. To say that the founders of the Seminary had a right to form and publicly avow their own religious principles; to say that they had a right to consecrate a portion of their property to the defense and diffusion of these principles, and to guard the sacred deposit against perversion as they have done in their statutes, is only to claim in their behalf a participation in the privileges common to every protestant and to every citizen of a free country." One individual who was active in the formation of the Pastoral Union and in measures immediately following did indeed favor a radical policy. No one, however, seconded his proposal to withdraw fellowship from the New School brethren. The intimate friends of Dr. Joseph Harvey could not have been surprised by his advocacy of an extreme measure. Excelled by few men in personal attractions, an able preacher and polemic, he inherited a morbid, nervous organization, that often taxed the patience of his friends, and best explains certain intellectual caprices that made him a doubtful coadjutor in any undertaking. At an early day he suddenly ceased to coöperate with the Pastoral Union and connected himself with the Presbyterian Church.

It has been well said that "earnestness and fidelity to convictions everywhere carry a cross." The men who conscientiously identified themselves with the Institute in its early days were well aware of the grave difficulties surrounding the enterprise. With few exceptions the press was either adverse or indifferent. Without a periodical to repel calumnious misrepresentations the trustees and faculty for the most part suffered in silence under the scourge of unscrupulous tongues and pens. The seclusion and incongenial surroundings of the Seminary, its moderate equipment in funds, books, teachers, and constituency offered abundant material to unfriendly critics. Their opportunity to prejudice the public mind was not lost. If a candidate for the gospel ministry set his face towards East Windsor, he did not fail to encounter warnings and dissuasives to which young men are keenly alive. That the number of students, compared with older seminaries, continued to be small was not surprising. That within the first few years thirty-four were in attendance was justly and devoutly recognized as a special token of divine favor. So also was their continuance, with so few exceptions, till the end of the course, in view of the odium that lessened their chance for a fair start in life. An early graduate after a long interval thus adverts to his experience: "Our numbers all told were few, and class distinctions, however informal and loosely held, narrowed still more the area of our restricted intimacies. Most of us were fresh from our large college associations with their varied excitements, and we found it hard to settle ourselves down into the narrow grooves in which our seminary life seemed to drag itself along. And the outside neighborhood was nearly as contracted as the Seminary. The families that cared for an acquaintance, though cultured and hospitable, were still infrequent and scattered. Both from within and from without a pressure was put upon us sometimes annoying and always troublesome. We were young men with aspirations for usefulness and ambitious of success. We were desirous to know and obey the truth, but at the same time did not want, if we could help it, to be put without the pale of popular sympathy and support." Gradually, as one small class after another came before ecclesiastical bodies for license or ordination, popular prejudice subsided. Judged by its average pupils it appeared that the Seminary was not belligerent, but contented itself with teaching the same evangelical truths that had long been the strength and inspiration of New England Congregational churches.

The limited views of our first Board of trustees were illustrated in two particulars. Instead of planning at the outset for a library that any competent judge would deem suitable for a public institution, they seemed to regard a few thousand volumes, chiefly such as could be spared from a pastor's study, as sufficient. The want of standard works in every department was a continued source of lamentation. In 1836, through the influence of Dr. John Todd, then pastor in Groton, Mass., one thousand dollars from the estate of Deacon Stone of Townshend was appropriated to the increase of the library. Not long after Mr. Abner Kingman of Boston Highlands, in gratitude that his pastor decided not to accept a professorship tendered him by the trustees of the Institute, made a handsome donation of carefully selected books neatly bound. Besides these gifts the trustees expended less than fifteen hundred dollars on the library during the thirty years prior to our leaving East Windsor Hill. The dreary record of three thousand volumes had indeed been changed to that of seven thousand before we came to Hartford. Of the fifty dollars allowed the librarian as his salary for forty-five years twenty-five dollars went to his assistant. Another sample of the humble standard with which the trustees were at first content may be seen in the annual income judged sufficient when the necessary buildings and other fixed property were paid for. In successive reports they expressed the opinion that three thousand dollars would defray current expenses. In partial justification of this estimate it should be known that one professor, who had received a handsome legacy from a rich brother in New York, served the institution gratuitously, and the salary of the youngest professor was six hundred and fifty dollars, exclusive of house rent. By some influential members of the board permanent funds were looked upon with distrust. Had they not in many cases been perverted? Are they not always a prize coveted by men seeking an easy position, and under little restraint from the obligations of creeds and the wills of deceased benefactors? "Let us shun this danger," said these good men. "We will rely on the annual gifts of those whose hearts are with us. Some of our own number will take short agencies, keeping the churches informed of our work, and thankfully accepting the smallest contributions." On a scale of three thousand dollars a year the plan seemed feasible. Its chief merit lay in securing from godly persons the prayers and sympathies not less helpful than their donations. The first year of the experiment was successful. Three hundred and twenty-eight subscribers were reported. The smallest sum in the list was fourteen cents, and the largest seven hundred and fifty dollars. Subscriptions were solicited chiefly in this state and in the city of New York. In the year 1839 a legacy of eleven thousand dollars was received from the estate of Miss Rebecca Waldo, of Worcester, Mass. This gift, by far the largest that had yet come into the treasury, was hailed with peculiar joy. Wide-spread commercial disasters had not long before crippled a number of our patrons, and the collection of three thousand dollars in small sums had already become a difficult task. From that time little was openly said against permanent endowments. Before a second professorship was in this way provided for, the moral support previously derived from Christian people in the humble walks of life sensibly declined. The annual subscribers numbering 328 in 1835 dropped down to seven in the year 1859.

Besides the one thousand dollars appropriated to the library by the trustees of Dea. Stone's estate in 1837, some years later Mr. Richard Bond of Boston Highlands bequeathed to the Institute seven thousand dollars, of which four thousand dollars were to be appropriated for the purchase of books. Besides the benefit of his professional services without compensation the Seminary received from Dr. Cogswell one thousand dollars towards the endowment of a Professorship of Ecclesiastical History, also liberal aid from time to time for the relief of needy students. At an early period in our history two thousand dollars were bequeathed to the Institute by Mr. Alva Gilman of Hartford. The joint bequest of the three Misses Waldo of Worcester, Mass., amounted to fourteen thousand dollars, and were set apart for the support of a Professor of Ecclesiastical History.

The second professorship placed upon a stable foundation was that of Christian Theology, by the bequest of Mr. Chester Buckley and his wife of Wethersfield. To the late Hon. Seth Terry the Institute is deeply indebted for the patience, tact, and legal experience, gratuitously employed in successfully thwarting an attempt to set aside the wills of Mr. and Mrs. Buckley. On becoming satisfied, after consulting the best legal authorities, that the validity of the wills was seriously endangered by a technical flaw, Judge Terry planned a compromise securing to the Seminary and various benevolent institutions a large proportion of the bequests named in the wills, and to the heirs-at-law a considerable amount in advance of what would have fallen to them by the terms of of the instrument in debate. The last of the three endowments furnished before the removal to Hartford came in part from the estate of the Rev. Dr. Asahel Nettleton. Besides a bequest for the support of the Professor of Bible Literature Dr. Nettleton left five hundred dollars for the purchase of periodicals, and whatever should be realized from the sales of Village Hymns for the benefit of indigent students. By a providential interposition the instrument bequeathing a portion of his property to charitable objects was preserved and its provisions executed. Grateful mention should be made of the assistance afforded our young brethren by yearly grants from the Hale Donation and the Everest Fund. From the former source between two and three hundred dollars, and from the latter at least fifty dollars, have been annually applied for this purpose. By means of scholarships a succession of young men have been helped on their way to the sacred office. Of these charitable foundations six were furnished before we came to Hartford and sixteen have been added since. The first in the series was the gift of Mr. Abner Kingman to perpetuate the memory of his respect and affection for Dr. Nehemiah Adams of Boston, and the second from the same liberal friend bearing the name of Eliot. The names of his beneficiaries were communicated from time to time to Mr. Kingman, so that he could follow them into their home or foreign fields. More than thirty years he had the satisfaction of seeing the fruit of this one species of his manifold beneficence. Our annals will faithfully transmit to coming generations the names of those whose gifts or services have made them prominent during the period just closed. But at least a word of grateful recognition is due to those self-sacrificing Christian women in Hartford and Tolland Counties, who ministered with patient toil, like Dorcas of old, to the wants of needy students from year to year. If unlike hers their names are unrecorded, they will have their reward.

The manual labor department of the Seminary was planned chiefly for the promotion of physical health, but some anticipated it would also yield pecuniary profit. Seventy acres of choice alluvial land, lying between the seminary buildings and Connecticut river, were purchased for tillage by students, and agricultural implements were furnished without charge. One acre or less, as he might choose, was allowed each student. The scheme included the construction of a road through the center of the field to the river, where a wharf was to be built to facilitate the transportation of farm products to this city. Operations began in the spring of 1834. The first gush of enthusiasm resulted in the construction of the road. A few, who had been accustomed to farm work in early youth, managed to keep in good health and earn enough to pay for a few text-books at the end of the season. As to the majority of the students, however, the outcome in respect both to health and profit was not altogether encouraging. In 1835 the net profit of work on land was two hundred and twelve dollars and seventy cents. In 1836, when the number of cultivators had increased, three hundred and eighty-three dollars and sixty-two cents were earned. The next year no estimate of proceeds was reported. Several drawbacks, not duly estimated at first, conspired to disappoint expectations from the agricultural branch of manual labor. As the soil became impoverished no provision was made for enriching it. Not unfrequently more time was required for necessary labor than fidelity to class-work would allow. As the terms of study were then arranged the summer vacation included one of the months when few crops can be wholly neglected without loss. Fortunately, as a home market was easily found for the products of the farm, no money was wasted on a wharf at the river. The fate of the workshop, intended for manual labor in cold and stormy weather, was even more disastrous. Each student was supplied with a box of tools, but with few exceptions the proper use of them was unknown to the young men. With no superintendent shop-tools rapidly depreciated in value, little merchantable work was produced, and the end of the experiment was much the same as of a similar one at Andover.

By their charter the trustees were authorized to establish a classical school as well as a theological seminary. Some of them were in favor of organizing it as early as 1836, but the majority declined taking any steps in that direction until their main enterprise had obtained firm footing. In 1850 public sentiment called with earnestness for the organization of a first-class academy. It was found that a large percentage of the pupils in the best training schools of Massachusetts were from Connecticut. There was evidently wanting among us a school sufficiently endowed to secure the services of well-qualified teachers, not dependent for support on tuition fees, and pledged to a high standard of scholarship irrespective of the number of pupils. This view was entertained by many who had no partiality for the East Windsor Institute. With the Pastoral Union and their associates the project found favor because it promised eventually to strengthen the higher institution under their care. Not that academical pupils would pass directly into the seminary, but some of them after leaving college would be predisposed to take their professional course in the place to which they had become attached in former years. By some of us the prospect of a good training school at our door was hailed as a welcome boon. It would solve a hard problem. If our children were to enjoy any better advantages than were offered by the very inferior schools of the town, how could their expenses away from home be met from an income of $650 a year? In 1851 the trustees took measures for putting into operation a classical school to bear the name of East Windsor Hill Academy. They avowed their purpose to provide both thorough instruction in the various branches of study and in the great principles of Christian faith. The direct superintendence of the academy was placed in the hands of a committee, two members of which were to be from the theological faculty. Mr. Paul A. Chadbourne was chosen principal, with an excellent corps of assistant teachers. Fifty pupils were in attendance the first year. The Assembly's Catechism was recited each week, and constant care was exercised to secure the objects dearest to the hearts of Christian parents. To this feature of the academy grateful tributes were paid in after years by the graduates. When Dr. Chadbourne was called to a professorship in Williams College his place could not be easily filled; but during the ten years of its existence the academy held to the purpose and pledge of its founders. Failing to obtain the funds required for the maintenance of its high standard, the trustees chose to discontinue the school rather than suffer its good name to be tarnished. Its graduates who entered our best colleges took a high rank, and keen disappointment was felt on all sides that pecuniary embarrassment had paralyzed a young training school in which centered so many hopes for the cause of accurate scholarship and high moral culture.

Although opposition to the Theological Seminary had declined as its spirit, methods, and results became known to the Christian public, and its pecuniary resources had at length reached a respectable figure, yet at the end of twenty years its guardians and friends became somewhat anxious. From the first local embarrassments had not been a slight obstacle to its growth. Instead of becoming less they had seriously increased. Facilities of intercourse between East Windsor Hill and other places had lessened. Steamboats had ceased to ply between Hartford and Springfield. The daily stage had been withdrawn. The railroad was on the opposite side of the river. To take a train one must go eight miles to Hartford or six to Warehouse Point or three to Windsor with the uncertainties of a primitive ferry. To or from either of these points no regular conveyance was established, and to obtain a private carriage was at times attended with difficulty. Dr. Eli Smith, the distinguished missionary, on a visit to his native land had occasion to find his way to East Windsor Hill in prosecution of a matrimonial alliance. In Springfield he learned that the nearest station was at Windsor. Stopping there at twilight he was a long time busy in finding a vehicle to take him to the river, where fresh delays and perils awaited the veteran traveler. On reaching his destination, he remarked, that in his various explorations in Palestine and Armenia he had experienced some inconveniences, but he never found it so difficult to get from one point to another as from Old Windsor to East Windsor Hill. Besides its isolation the seminary suffered from want of social and spiritual vitality and a literary atmosphere so helpful to studious young men.

From 1855 to 1860 the Institution passed through a trying ordeal. For reasons already adverted to in part its continued existence was debated by its stanchest friends. While the academy continued to flourish, such was the decline in the theological department of the Institute as to threaten at least its temporary suspension. To guard the funds in such an emergency became an object of solicitude with the Trustees. Under legal advice it was decided that, if one of the theological professors should serve temporarily as principal of the school, the funds of the Institute would not be forfeited. Accordingly the Professor of Biblical Literature was requested to act in that capacity. This arrangement, involving no addition to the Professor's salary, was an economical one, as it saved to the treasury the amount otherwise required for the support of a principal. The proposal was accepted and several hours were daily spent in the academy without curtailing the time allotted to Hebrew and Greek in the other building. To instruct advanced classes fitting for college required of the teacher a review of the branches quite neglected for thirty years. This style of labor continued for two years.

Meanwhile the trustees of the Institute invited the corporators of Yale College to consider an overture for uniting the two seminaries. The number of students in each was small and declining. The guardians of each were constrained to ask what could forestall the calamity that threatened both. The proposed conference took place between a committee of our trustees and the Prudential Committee and afterwards the Clerical Fellows of Yale College. On both sides, it would seem, the conference was candid and courteous. Our trustees signified to the other party "that they had in charge three sacred and inalienable trusts; their funds, their faith, and a school in which these funds should be devoted to the inculcation of their faith." They asked therefore to be received into the united seminary in their complete and unrestrained integrity. It was proposed that the united school should be at New Haven; that the present professors in both seminaries should retire, leaving all the chairs to be filled by a new election; that the trustees of the Institute should nominate candidates and the Corporation should have power to elect, but only from among these nominees. These were the chief points. To all the specifications of the overture the New Haven gentlemen acceded, with one exception. They demurred as to the mode of appointing professors, and proposed as a substitute that a union be formed substantially upon the basis already set forth, except that, instead of the trustees of the Pastoral Union nominating and the Corporation of the College electing the professors, the boards should constitute distinct and independent houses of convocation, each electing, and that a concurrent election shall be necessary in each case to actual induction. While offering this as a basis of prospective union the New Haven gentlemen signified that a due regard to certain very obvious personal relations and sympathies compelled them to ask a delay of definite action until such time as Providence should seem to indicate. After the conferences closed two of the Clerical Fellows of the Corporation signified that they should require some restriction upon the creed of the Pastoral Union if it was to be enforced in the united seminary. The attempt at union thus proving futile our board of trustees in 1856 summoned the friends of the Institute to "instant and earnest and assiduous endeavor and united prayer to God" for the increase of its efficiency. Only partial success, however, attended the efforts thus called forth. · Local hindrances to the growth of the Seminary became more and more formidable from year to year. In the judgment of many its continued life depended upon its being transplanted to a more eligible home. Prominent trustees came to their annual meetings after 1857 with feelings little akin to a joyous reunion. Still the majority of the board were nothing daunted by the untoward signs which were hailed with joy by those whose maxim from the first had been; "Delenda est Carthago." How to effect an escape from our paralyzing environments and rekindle the languishing hopes of guardians and friends came to be an urgent problem. To leave East Windsor Hill was to incur a considerable loss of property, to inflict a deep wound upon certain liberal and steadfast friends who could not listen to arguments in favor of a removal from the old site, and to run the risk of extinction elsewhere in circumstances of mortifying publicity.

In the early part of this transitional period of our history the infirmities of age compelled Dr. Tyler to ask a release from his official trusts. Before his resignation and to the last day of his life his prevailing belief and hope were that the Institute would see brighter days. Occasionally, indeed, he yielded for a moment to a feeling of despondence and once or twice read at evening prayers in the chapel the hymn; "By whom shall Jacob now arise, for Jacob's friends are few." Without warning and without the slightest justification anonymous charges against his doctrinal soundness were put in circulation just as he was leaving a post which he had honorably filled for more than twenty years. This bitter cup, it is supposed, was prepared by a few members of the Pastoral Union who had shared with him the burdens of an unpopular undertaking. Brooding over the misfortune which seemed to threaten the beloved Seminary they yielded to the suspicion that the Professor of Theology was the Achan that troubled the camp. At an informal trial which was forced upon the Pastoral Union the charges in question were thoroughly refuted and the way made clear for the venerable professor to retire with dignity and grace.

In 1864 the Clerical Fellows of Yale College appointed a committee, of which the late Dr. Hawes was chairman, to confer with our trustees on the question of uniting the two seminaries. Since the abortive attempt in the same direction in 1856 such changes had taken place as awakened fresh hope that the measure might be consummated. But it was destined to a second and final defeat. The trustees of the Institute had now resolved to remove it to Hartford "in order to open to it a wider field of usefulness and to confer upon it greater privileges." This step was agreed upon in spite of their disappointment in the effort to raise a fund of two hundred thousand dollars, deemed necessary to meet the increased outlay required by the proposed change. At the meeting of the Pastoral Union that year (1864) statements were made by ministerial brethren, from Massachusetts which favored an enlargement of our constituency beyond the bounds of the state of Connecticut. The brethren from a neighboring state expressed a desire to coöperate with us in checking the speculations of a false philosophy which had invaded the denomination, and which they deemed more alarming at that time than ever before. In consequence of the representations and appeals made at that juncture the Union passed several resolutions favoring an invitation to its membership of any Congregational pastors in sympathy with our theological sentiments. Up to this time the Pastoral Union embraced few ministers not living in Connecticut. At present a considerable number from other states are enrolled among its members. The first accession from Massachusetts rendered much assistance in the removal to Hartford, but, subsequently less aid than was expected came from that particular band of allies. By more than one of their number it was confidently affirmed that, if a pastor in eastern Massachusetts were elected to a professorship in the Seminary, funds would be supplied from that quarter for his salary. The election was made but no funds came from " Boston and vicinity." To meet the embarrassment that ensued our steadfast patron, Mr. James B. Hosmer, gave fifty thousand dollars for the support of the new Massachusetts Professor. That the receipts of the treasury might equal its expenditures Mr. Hosmer had been accustomed as treasurer to make good the annual deficits from his own resources, but in view of the circumstances this gift of fifty thousand dollars revealed a magnanimity of character not less worthy of record than the still larger donations reserved for a later day. While the Seminary was adjusting itself to its new surroundings schemes for its amalgamation with two western seminaries were set on foot. At the meeting of the National Council in Oberlin in 1871 an effort was made to enlist the moral support of that body in carrying out this policy. A series of resolutions was offered, one of which read as follows: "That we recognize thankfully the valuable service which the Theological Seminary at Hartford has done in the past and that we heartily commend its system of instruction, but in view of the fact that two institutions of a similar character are no longer needed in close proximity to each other its consolidation with one of the western seminaries, if such a measure be practicable, would be viewed with satisfaction by our churches, and would, we believe, greatly enlarge its sphere of usefulness." From another western institution a proposal was made to receive us, doctrines, funds, teachers and all. From still another quarter came indefinite overtures of the same kind. Certainly the proposed method of dispatching a troublesome life was more adroit, if it proved no more successful, than the somewhat violent one encountered in its infancy. Its persistence, however, and symptoms of fresh vigor in its new home were accepted at length as providential signs that it had a mission of its own this side the Allegheny Mountains. The sixth and last attempt to put an end to the independent existence of the Institute took the form of an anonymous pamphlet entitled, "Can it be done?" No intelligent reader of the document could doubt its authorship or the plausibility of its reasoning. In point of time it had the advantage of appearing while we occupied hired dwelling houses on Prospect Street, not altogether adapted to our use, and suggestive of a second migration. The distinguished writer of the missive sent it to each Congregational minister in Connecticut, not, he says, "with any purpose of introducing a public discussion of the subject or expecting that its suggestions would be at once unanimously approved, but with the hope that in due season they would bear some fruit." The chief obstacle which he foresaw in the way of merging our Seminary in that at New Haven lay in the subscription to our creed, but he fondly hoped that a rigorous exactness would not be insisted upon, so that the formulary could be adopted by all who recognize in a general way the doctrines common to the various Protestant confessions. He presents the form of a compact intended to secure the rights and endowments of both institutions.

MY COLLEAGUES.

At first and for several years there were but three professors. Dr. Tyler was a graduate of Yale College, studied his profession with Rev. Asahel Hooker of Goshen, and was pastor in Middlebury, Conn., till called to the presidency of Dartmouth College. On resigning that post he succeeded Dr. Edward Payson as pastor at Portland, and in 1834 was chosen Professor of Theology in our seminary. His literary and professional attainments were about the same as those of Dr. Ebenezer Porter of Andover, Dr. Humphrey, President of Amherst College, and Dr. Lyman Beecher. Our records speak none too highly of his great worth and valuable services. His clear, logical method in argument, "his sound judgment, his love of the great doctrines of the Gospel, his eminent ability to teach and defend them, his warm, devoted, and uniform piety, the generosity of his heart, and the urbanity of his manner, admirably qualified him for his office." It was well said that "the success of the Institute in its early struggles was in no small measure to be ascribed under God to his hopeful spirit, his unwavering faith, his firmness and courage, his untiring and unselfish efforts." I labored with him as a son with a father from 1834 to 1858. The native kindness of his disposition, his self-control and practical wisdom made him a delightful companion, while he was *facile princeps* among the guardians and teachers of the Seminary.

Dr. Jonathan Cogswell, our first Professor of Ecclesiastical History, was graduated at Harvard College, preached some years in Saco, Maine, and when the Institute was founded, was pastor of the First Church in New Britain. A legacy from his brother in New York enabled him to tender his services to the trustees without cost to the Seminary. His generosity and good nature checked the adverse criticisms to which his professional services were sometimes liable.

From its commencement Dr. Asahel Nettleton held a semi-official relation to the Institute. Owing to precarious health he spent the winter months in Virginia, where he had labored in revivals with signal success. As an inmate of my family for several months, always considerate of the feelings and welfare of those about him, by the serenity of his countenance, his animated and instructive conversation, and by his entire deportment, so humble, gentle, and in every way magnetic, he won our profound respect and ardent affection. In spite of the deep sand through which the road lay from Hartford to East Windsor Hill many an old friend found his way to Dr. Nettleton's residence to renew personal friendships or to confer with him relative to the kingdom of Christ. At the time when he was attacked by the malady of which he died after protracted sufferings, he was living with his brother a short distance from the Seminary. His familiar lectures to the students on revivals so long as he was able to meet them, as well as his occasional sermons in the Chapel, were highly valued. Students of that day will never forget his visits at their rooms for conversation on spiritual themes usually closing with prayer. With the avails of Village Hymns he had bought a house and farm at East Windsor Hill for the use of an indigent brother with whom he planned to spend the evening of life. Almost daily visits for more than a year, and at least a score of nights of watching at his bedside, justify the testimony now given, that neither racking pains nor nameless social trials, from which a sensitive nature shrinks, extorted from his lips a word of complaint. In the last fiery ordeal the Christian graces, so conspicuous in the prime of his public life, shone with unwonted lustre.

Dr. Nahum Gale, who succeeded Dr. Cogswell in the chair of Ecclesiastical History, was much younger than either of my other colleagues. He had been at the Institute as a pupil, and came to his office from a thriving pastorate in Ware, Mass. After two or three years Professor Gale became doubtful of the continuance of the Seminary and accepted an invitation to settle as pastor of the Church in Lee, Mass., where he labored successfully till his death.

In 1844 Dr. Edward Hooker, then pastor in Bennington, Vt., was elected Professor of Homiletics and Pastoral Duty, and continued in office four years. He was a greatgrandson of President Edwards, and a son of Rev. Asahel Hooker of Goshen, with whom Dr. Tyler and other useful ministers had studied theology near the beginning of the present century, before the Seminary at Andover was founded. The families of Drs. Tyler and Hooker formed a group exceptionally amiable and refined. Dr. Hooker enjoyed the respect and affectionate sympathy of his brethren and pupils in his labors and repeated afflictions. He served with conscientious fidelity in his appointed sphere, but his partiality for the pastoral office led to his resignation at the end of four years.

Our third Professor of Church History was Rev. Dr. Edward A. Lawrence. Since his recent death his talents, scholarship, and character have called out warm and discriminating eulogies from those who knew little of his work with us. Before he came to the Seminary and during the twenty years after he withdrew from it he impressed all who knew him with the accuracy, thoroughness, and extent of his knowledge, the firmness of his convictions, his courtesy, fairness, and candor; his modesty, gentleness, and fidelity to every trust. His uniform serenity and self-poise under sore provocations were among the many proofs that he held frequent communion with his divine Master. To his yearning spirit heaven seemed more and more but another name for uninterrupted and eternal fellowship with his Lord.

"There is a sight from men concealed;
That sight, the face of God revealed,
Shall bless the pure in heart."

Of my eight colleagues who have finished their course, only one more will be named in this sketch. To the citizens of Hartford Dr. Robert G. Vermilye was better known than either of my associates of whom mention has been made. When the Institution came to this city in 1865, he was one of the two Professors constituting the faculty. That trying period of our history brought into clear light the noble qualities of his character. But want of time forbids more than a glance at his characteristics. For Christian integrity and kindness, unswerving loyalty to Gospel truth with fairness to opponents, for refined dignity on public occasions and in the ordinary intercourse of life, for the rare union of qualities denoted by the true friend, the Christian gentleman, the able divine, the accomplished teacher and preacher, both the pupils and colleagues of Dr. Vermilye will cherish his memory with affection and respect.

Among the founders and devoted friends of the Seminary Rev. George A. Calhoun deserves to be held in grateful remembrance. For more than forty years pastor in North Coventry he acquired an enviable reputation both among his own people and the churches of the state. His good judgment, his intelligent apprehension of the issues involved in the discussions raised by the New Haven divines, his charitable temper and prudent speech qualified him for the prominent position long held as trustee of the Institute. To him specially fell the task of collecting in small sums the funds to meet current expenses before endowments were provided. His tall, well-proportioned figure, the benignant seriousness of his countenance, his slow movements and deliberate speech invited the confidence and respect felt by all who knew him. His influence, it is believed, secured an early appropriation, repeated annually while he lived, by the trustees of the Hale Donation in aid of our students. Very few of them were able to defray current expenses from their own funds, and the Hale charity was eminently opportune. The whole amount received from that source and appropriated to reduce the cost of board is found to be $12,310.

One of the most remarkable men connected with the early history of the Institute was Nathaniel Hewitt, D.D. At the time of its organization he was pastor of a church in Bridgeport. Some years before that his name had become familiar to the country as the "Apostle of Temperance." His overwhelming assaults on the drinking usages of those days made him famous in 1827, but his power as a pulpit orator had already achieved signal results in Fairfield. In any assembly he would impress a casual observer as an uncommon man. His massive form crowned with an imperial head, his features bearing the stamp of a lofty, determined spirit, his voice equally suited to the son of thunder and the son of consolation, were a part of his rare native gifts. With the traits that command admiration and respect were united others of a gentler kind that won the warmest affection of intimate companions. In his better frames, even when past the meridian of life, his conversational powers fascinated any circle of youth or reverend seniors. As a pastor in ministering to the afflicted and such as were oppressed with spiritual trouble his sympathy and skill were as noteworthy as the stronger features of his character on public occasions. Dr. Hewitt's theological convictions were entwined indissolubly with his personal religious experience. Deep consciousness of sin and assurance of salvation through the expiatory sufferings of Christ made it easy for him to accept the distinctive teachings of the New Testament and impelled him to preach and defend them most loyally. No one probably had more influence than Dr. Hewitt in the establishment of our Seminary, and for several years he labored earnestly for its welfare. Always punctual in his attendance at the anniversaries, and not an infrequent visitor at other times, the family that secured him for a guest or even at a dinner was deemed fortunate.

For thirty-three years the pastorate of Dr. Elisha Lord Cleveland in New Haven was coincident with the life of the Seminary at East Windsor. As a trustee, he was identified with it for about a quarter of a century, and in the fellowship of long-continued trials for conscience sake, mutual sympathy bound us very closely together. It was natural that the youngest teacher in the Institute and its youngest trustee should be on the most intimate terms. Classmates at Andover, of the same age, favored with similar home-training in early life, traditionally and experimentally partial to the faith of the primitive churches held by our fathers, we could not differ widely respecting theological novelties that startled and distressed reverent students of the divine Word. Dr. Cleveland went to New Haven after graduating at Andover for the purpose of gaining such additional preparation for the work of the ministry as the eminent teacher in the theological department of Yale College might afford. Soon called by the Third Church to become its pastor, he took a firm stand in relation to the doctrinal controversy then at its height. His church and congregation, neither rich nor numerous at the time of his settlement, were deeply in debt for their place of worship. The creditors, displeased with the doctrinal views set forth by the young pastor, pressed their claim so vigorously that he with his little flock that clung to him retired to an obscure hall. A feeble band despised by the world, they went forth from their house of worship welcoming the reproach and embarrassment sure to follow. Fidelity to the principles he had avowed and taught seemed to require that the pastor should face any trial that the Master might appoint him when called to act so conspicuously as the representative of a conservative theology. "He cast his lot with poverty, odium, and the inevitable loss for a period of public and social position in the cultivated circles of a literary and ecclesiastical center, in which he had been a favorite, and which he was so well fitted to grace and enjoy." At length the little band that worshiped in a hall became a large, wealthy, and intelligent congregation. Their hall was exchanged first for the lecture-room kindly offered them by the Center Church, then for a new church edifice, attractive and commodious, and at last for the stately and beautiful temple which now adorns a central locality in the City of Elms. From a mere pittance the pastor's salary became the most liberal in the city. "He was sought to officiate on high public occasions." "His voice was heard more impressive and effective than any other," says Dr. Bacon, "in the great assembly of citizens that was convened at New Haven to pledge their support to the imperiled government." "In aid of his inward resources and endowments for high oratory and eloquence came all that richness, pathos, and melody of voice, so familiar to his congregation. There was his broad, yet not disproportioned frame, his face of singular beauty and strength, his deep-set eye, instinct with intelligence, at times almost hidden under his massive, overhanging brow, often and not unjustly likened to Daniel Webster's; the whole so apt to be lighted up by that smile which loved to play upon his lips, and which, if less than seraphic, often seemed more than human." Time permits only the bare mention of his executive ability, prudence, firmness, the amiability of his temper, the wisdom, gentleness, and benignity, which shed such a radiance over his own home and made him so welcome in the families of his parishioners.

Not by way of complaint, but as an instance of the limitations under which the interior work of the Institute was carried on, a glance is due at a single personal experience for a considerable period from the year 1834. Lack of funds and possibly defective views of what is implied in the phrase Biblical Literature may explain the fact that one individual was made responsible for all the teaching furnished the students in the exegesis both of the Old Testament and the New. By general consent first-rate scholarship and leisurely training are indispensable requisites for success in either of these branches. Everybody would now say, if you would overwhelm the teacher and inflict an irreparable injury on his scholars, give him both. To my gray-haired pupils now before me, who must have often lamented the poor quality of their exegetical instruction at East Windsor Hill, I can only say the fault was not wholly mine. It is also remembered that the Professor of Hebrew and Greek was not at liberty to give his undivided strength to the work officially assigned him. At an early day a church was organized in the Seminary, which was located two miles from any place of worship, and two sermons were preached in the chapel every Sabbath. The service came to each of the Professors once in three weeks. Two of them had been pastors more than a score of years, the third just one year. The inevitable effect of this arrangement need not be described. Another little drawback should be mentioned. Among the extra official duties not to be evaded was the superintendence of rhetorical exercises and the correction of one-third of the sermons required from members of the senior class. At a later day the department of Church History became vacant. With the help of textbooks the Professor of Biblical Literature served for a time as a proxy. A little further on, when the health of the theological Professor broke down, the man of all work, now no longer young, was requested to take up for a time a part of the burden which had fallen from Dr. Vermilye's hands. Two prizes of sixty dollars each were offered about the year 1858 to members of the middle and senior classes who should pass the best examination in the first and second volumes of Turrettin's Theology. No member of the faculty coveted the office of examiner who must be supposed ready to try his pupils on any one of twelve hundred pages of ecclesiastical Latin. A majority vote of the professors added this to the other multifarious duties of the Professor of Biblical Literature. It was well for him that among Mr. Kingman's gifts to the library was a copy of *Forcellini totius Latinitatis Lexicon* in four royal quarto volumes. Without this aid he might have hesitated one time to examine the valedictorian of his class at Yale College, who easily won the Turrettin prize.

From necessity the proper division of labor, if theoretically acknowledged, was practically postponed to a recent period in our history. If one "thrust himself into the duties or usurp the office of another," let the law of mutual subserviency exact a fit penalty. But if the foot does not volunteer to attempt the work of the hand, doing the ungracious thing under an iron necessity, "he is more sinned against than sinning." In commenting on the distribution of service enjoined in the twelfth chapter of Romans, Chalmers utters a protest against the modern policy of the church, a policy not unknown in other organizations. "We should as much as possible," he says, "humor, even as the Spirit Himself does, the constitutional varieties of tastes and talent among men. . . . . . The tendency now is in an opposite direction and each has many things laid upon him. . . . . . What makes it all the more ruinous is, that rarely indeed is one man eminent in more than one thing; and the sure way, therefore, of degrading him from eminence to mediocrity is to bustle and belabor him with more than one thing."

The review allotted me to-day may suitably close with a reference to two or three contrasts fitted to inspire with gratitude and large expectations the guardians and friends of our Seminary. The number of students connected with the Institution during the thirty years prior to its removal from East Windsor never ran higher than thirty-four. Sometimes it fell much lower. Our present catalogue contains fifty-four names. The library has grown from three thousand to thirty-eight thousand volumes. This numerical difference is fully equalled by the difference in the quality of our literary treasures. Less than two thousand dollars was laid out for books during our first three decades. To our earnest plea for help in that direction scarcely a faint response came back. At length a generous patron has appeared and the days of our mourning are ended. His name will be held in lasting and grateful remembrance by a long succession of teachers and pupils. Another mural tablet will not be wanting in our Hall when he is taken hence.

In one particular a serious loss attended our removal to this city. Instead of the convenient, well-lighted, and well-ventilated rooms at the old home, our apartments in three dwelling-houses in Prospect street, and for a time in a fourth on Main street, were far from being satisfactory. Between the fifteen years passed in such quarters and the last five in this edifice we observe another step in our onward movement. Representatives of any class from 1834 to 1840, who may be here to-day, must remember the anniversary occasions of that period. The lecture-room, used also as a chapel, would accommodate besides the faculty, students and trustees not more than fifty persons. Addresses by members of the graduating class and by some eminent divine, it is presumed, were heard with satisfaction and profit by all present. Among the friends of the Seminary in neighboring towns were some excellent singers who conducted the service of song at these annual gatherings, assisted by the home choir. On one occasion, owing probably to the absence of outside helpers, the musical part of the entertainment seemed likely to be a failure. But unexpected help was at hand. A young man from an obscure hill-town had found his way into the chapel. He had enjoyed such advantages for the cultivation of music as the village singing schools of that day afforded, and seizing the opportunity to volunteer a solo when a suitable interval occured, he sung in a heavy bass voice the entire hymn of Mrs. Hemans on the landing of the Pilgrims. Over against that performance will be given this evening the Oratorio of the Messiah by the Hosmer Hall Choral Union.

Financially the outlay of three thousand dollars a year has grown, probably, to seven or eight times that sum, and authority given at first to hold fifty thousand dollars' worth of property now covers the right to hold twenty times this amount. As to the method of making the column of receipts tally with that of disbursements, it is surmised that between our present treasurer and his predecessor it would not be easy to picture a contrast. Estimated by a just standard, the title of collegiate and theological institutions to public confidence depends on their teachers far more than on their material resources and accommodations. The advance made by our Seminary in this vital matter is a plain token of "the good will of Him that dwelt in the bush." This comparison of then and now should embrace one more feature. The sneers and unscrupulous censures, leveled at our Institute in its youth and its long struggle with poverty and weakness, have largely given way either to a decent silence or words of confidence and cheer. This happy change is distinctly shown also by liberal gifts, increasing sympathy and other tokens of regard from our fellow-citizens, which we trust the future will more and more justify.

Only in rare instances is one permitted to look back and note the vicissitudes of an enterprise with which his hopes and toils have been identified for half a century, from early manhood to quite beyond three score years and ten. Of the thirty-six men who met in the small brick school-house at East Windsor fifty years ago only three are now living. Of the first board of trustees, twenty-four in number, not one remains. Of the eight Professors who held office while we continued at East Windsor Hill I am the only one left. At short intervals the names on our Historical Catalogue are marked with the lethal star.

But the Seminary abides. The tree transplanted from East Windsor to Prospect and from Prospect to Broad street without being killed or dwarfed may be expected to outlive successive generations of trustees, professors, and pupils. The badge seen on the walls of an old English mansion, long occupied by the family of Moore, is the mulberry tree, the *morus*, and the legend is, "*Morus tarde moriens, morum cito moritur.*" The mulberry tree is slow to die; the mulberry fruit dies soon. Outside of our city and of our commonwealth friendly eyes are directed to this seat of sacred learning. •If we hesitate to credit the predictions of sanguine coadjutors who have recently espoused our cause, yet they may well incite us to whole-hearted endeavors in our allotted field. When devout, scholarly interpretation of the divine Word, based on approved principles, shall fail to sanction any doctrine here taught—when theological novelties antagonistic to the faith of the Christian Church for ages shall have vindicated themselves in personal purity and spiritual fruitfulness hitherto unknown or rarely witnessed—it will be soon enough to revise our creed. Tested by the best biblical scholarship, by countless individual experiences and by their transforming, elevating power on domestic, social, and national life, let the doctrines which we hold and teach ever find able advocates and cordial friends in the guardians and faculty of this Institution.

Our Seminary began its life as a practical protest against what were deemed unscriptural sentiments. Like the speckled bird of the prophet, "the birds round about were against her." If others judge that the time has come to exchange signals with those who deny the supreme authority of the Scriptures, the expiatory nature of Christ's death, and the endless punishment of those who die impenitent, let us incur a fresh storm of obloquy, if need be, and welcome double the distresses of past years rather than prove disloyal to the faithful and true Witness. Should some ingenious rationalistic speculator attempt to use our consecrated funds for purposes alien to the views inculcated here for the last half century, let the memory of Tyler and Nettleton, of Atwater, Calhoun, and Hosmer rouse their official successors to the fearless discharge of their sacred trust. If the gratified sentiment that pervades our present convocation is shared by invisible spectators, let us hope that the enlarged cloud of witnesses at our next jubilee may rejoice that the Hartford Theological Seminary is permitted to bear a humble part in whatever service may be needful at that brighter day to complete the triumph of Christ our Lord. Mindful of the perils that beset all human organizations we will rely on the guardianship of Him who has been our helper in all the checkered history of the past. "The Lord our God be with us as He was with our fathers; let Him not leave us nor forsake us; that He may incline our hearts unto Him, to walk in all His ways, and to keep His commandments, and His statutes, and His judgments which He commanded our fathers," to Whom be glory and honor, thanksgiving and praise.

Bennett Tyler, D.D.

BY REV. LAVALETTE PERRIN, D. D.

·I have been requested to give a pen-picture appropriate to this occasion of Rev. Bennett Tyler, DD., as he stands related to the work of this Seminary, and to polemic theology in New England. While I appreciate the complimentary courtesy of the request, I am at a loss to find in myself any special fitness for such a service, unless it be that given by the opportunity while studying theology, and during the early years of my ministry, to observe from an unbiased stand-point, the parties to a vigorous polemic struggle which was happily issued in the victory of both.

If it had been required of my now sainted mother, whose relations to this Institution in its early struggles were quite intimate, to characterize Dr. Tyler as a man, a neighbor, a minister, a preacher, and a pastor, I am sure she would have done it, in the use of all proper terms of admiration and eulogy, in the superlative degree. And to her estimate I should heartily subscribe, first from a belief that no more conscientious and competent witness could be called, and also because a limited personal acquaintance gave the same testimony.

This service does not require the expression of personal or partisan devotion. Nor should this occasion be used for the parade of fulsome eulogy. If the praise wrought so often into the rhetoric of commemorative discourse, were expressed in loving, helpful fellowship with living workers in their toils and trials, death might sometimes defer his advent among them. A larger charity, and a more sympathizing, coöperative zeal among the living, will serve the cause of the Master better than incense burned upon the tombs of the dead. We are indeed to cherish the memory of the just, but our regard for God's servants should not begin at their graves. It is a fault of our times that living, struggling worth, is often lost sight of in the shadow of departed greatness, real or illusive.

The chief value of commemorative discourse to the earnest Christian worker, is in the aid it gives him for the study of God's providential provision for the spread and defense of the truth. It is both instructive and inspiring to observe how, for the development and spread of His Kingdom, God raises up the needed human agents at the right time. Studied in this light, the biography of eminent Christian scholars and workers is as profitable as it is interesting. In this light let us try to set the character and work of Dr. Tyler.

The eighteenth century is remarkable for certain preparatory movements and provisions for the wonderful developments of the nineteenth. This is as true in the religious as it is in the political history of our country and the world. As when on a summer's day which precedes some great convulsion of nature, the skilled observer discerns tokens of coming agitation in the cast of the sky, the state of the atmosphere, and the fleecy mists that rise here and there, so in the religious aspect of the New England churches during the eighteenth century, the discriminating observer sees a divine preparation for that signal outcome of mental and spiritual activity, which has given us two flourishing theological seminaries in the State of Connecticut, and a rapid succession of new departures in the methods and matter of Christian teaching.

In their utter rejection of the petrified forms of godliness, the churches in the middle of the last century had well-nigh lost the power of godliness, which always requires some form for its proper exercise and expression. The necessities of their case, and their isolated condition, had fostered a hard, materialistic tendency in modes of thought, and the theology of the times had little power to stir and lift the soul. The logic of the intellect had so crystalized about the technics of the day as to allow no exercise for the rhetoric of the feelings. A revolution was to be effected in the thought-systems and forms of the New England churches. The raw, cheerless, dead air of a necessitarian philosophy was to give place to a more genial, life-inspiring atmosphere. Only a thunder-storm that should sweep the entire realm of religious thought, and leave echoes and reverberations here and there skirting the horizon for long years to come, would sift its deadly elements from the moral atmosphere, and give it moisture and vitalizing energy.

God works in the spiritual world as truly as in the natural, by laws and agents adapted to the end in view. In the line of this thought is a fact worthy of our special notice just here. The eighteenth century produced, in these New England churches, a number of stalwart Christian thinkers, and the first half of the present century was marked by the appearance of just that conflict of opinion which is incidental to real progress, in the apprehension of spiritual truth. Without naming others, of whom there were many, we may notice six eminent divines who may be said to have prepared the way for, and contributed largely to, that battle of the bishops which was in progress fifty years ago—called by one writer the "Connecticut Controversy," and some of the veterans in which were just resting upon their laurels when I entered the ministry. Let me name them in the order of their birth, and do not fail to observe that five of them were natives of our little State, and the sixth did his life-work in it. Jonathan Edwards was born at Windsor in 1703; Joseph Bellamy at New Cheshire in 1719; Samuel Hopkins at Waterbury in 1721; Nathaniel Emmons at East Haddam in 1745; Timothy Dwight at Northampton in 1752; and Charles G. Finney at Warren in 1792. These names are as household words in the discussions and Christian activities of the present century. Beginning with Jonathan Edwards, who wrestled with the mighty problem of sin and salvation while teaching savages in the wilderness, and closing with Charles G. Finney, who swept the broad and barren field of logical skepticism with the fire of a new spiritual life, the last century gave birth to the efficient agents in a grand movement forward and upward of Christian thought and purpose.

The progress has been slow, and some of the steps in it have seemed for a time to be backward rather than forward, but viewed as a whole the trend of thought and feeling has been steadily in advance. From 1750 to 1850 we easily trace the steps of progress toward this result, and this Institution is an incidental product of the transition process.

Already had the sturdy logic of Edwards, blended with the facile rhetoric of Dwight, and fired with the fervor, aggressive zeal and questioned methods of Finney, brought on an irrepressible conflict of views and utterances, when I first became a servant of the churches. A host of Christian champions were wrestling with the new thought-forms which the spirit of progress demanded. To me, then, they seemed like giants, and I doubt not they were honestly, as they certainly were earnestly, contending for the faith once delivered to the saints. The rank and file of our Connecticut ministers recognized as worthy leaders such men as Dow of Thomson, Yale of New Hartford, Cleveland of New Haven, Hewett of Bridgeport, Calhoun of Coventry, Nettleton the Evangelist, and Perkins of West Hartford, who did not fully agree with Porter of Farmington, McEwen of New London, Goodrich of New Haven, Bushnell of Hartford, Bacon of New Haven, and Arms of Norwich, in the choice of terms and methods to be used in their work. These valiant soldiers, with others of equal worth and ability, too numerous to name in this brief sketch, were in active service on the field, when, as a raw recruit, I entered the ranks on duty. Noble men they were, loyal to the Master, and seeking the spread of truth, but having gifts differing and seeing the truth under different phases or aspects, it quite naturally followed that some of the words they employed were not fitly chosen, and not always fitly spoken. But we trust they have all now entered those realms of light and harmony, where they see as they are seen and know as they are known, and these differences by which they were so disturbed in the flesh have melted away in the light and warmth of the Sun of Righteousness.

We have thus a background upon which to set the picture of Dr. Tyler. It will doubtless seem to you that the background is made the chief feature of the picture. There are two reasons for this. First, the face itself has been already drawn in his published memoir, to which, as a portrait of the man himself, I cannot hope to add, and which you would not wish me to repeat. And secondly, to get a right view of the man we must see him as he was encircled by the earnest Christian men of his day, intent upon what seemed to them a momentous issue. Upon this background he rises before us, the central figure of a school or phalanx, over against whom, in a like aspect of leadership, was Dr. Taylor of New Haven. It was my privilege as a student to sit at the feet of both, and it is my pleasure here to express a high admiration of them, as able, honest, and earnest teachers and preachers of the gospel of Jesus Christ. Differing widely in mental structure and furniture, each possessed a special fitness for the position he occupied on the battle-field of the hour. Taking their observations from different stand-points, it was natural that they should emphasize different truths, and different phases of the same truth. It brings out the features of Dr. Tyler more minutely to mark the difference between the two. In both there is reverence for the truth, and zeal in proclaiming it. In one it is reverence for the truth as formulated by the fathers. In the other it is reverence for the truth as personally apprehended. With Dr. Tyler there was something valuable in old associations. He loved not only truth, but the familiar dress which it wore. Besides, he was distrustful of human speculations. With him faith had no need of philosophy as a voucher. Not what man can comprehend, but what God has revealed, was with him the ruling question. Yet he would retain and use the old technical terms as the signs of living ideas, not as the monuments of dead ones. Nor would he allow rhetorical beauties to harden into logical perplexities. To know and teach the truth as revealed in the word of God was his guiding purpose. While partial to the old terms and methods, he was not blind to new aspects of truth and new expressions for it. Indeed, so kindly did he carry himself toward any improvement in this respect, that at one time he fell under the suspicion of favoring the "new departure" of his day, and was under formal surveillance by certain strict constructionists, as tending to a departure from the faith. Nor is it difficult to see by a comparison of his earliest with his latest writings, that his own views of truth were modified and enlarged by his study and criticism of the views of others. But his loyalty to the word of God was unfeigned and steadfast.

With our canvas and its background thus prepared, if we view Dr. Tyler in a comparison with others,—say Drs. Taylor, Hewett, Goodrich, Calhoun, and Porter of Farmington, it will help us to get the more important features of the man. While he differed from each of these in character as a whole, he combined their leading features in well-rounded and happily-balanced harmony. The adventurous assurance of Taylor; the dictatorial push of Hewett; the quick zeal of Goodrich; the stern conservatism of Calhoun; and the winning benevolence of Porter, make striking personal contrasts when put in bold relief and distinct outline upon the same canvas. But the Divine Artist so wrought the extremes of these virtuous impulses into a golden mean of true saintliness in the character of Dr. Tyler, that his face alone upon the picture gives us their embodied harmony. This happy combination of qualities fitted him for the special relation in which he stood to this institution, and to the churches and ministers of his time.

As a man he was well furnished, and of comprehensive affinities for all the relations of life. The well-ordered Christian family was to him an earthly paradise. There, in all the quiet beauty and loveliness of chastened piety, he scattered benedictions and was refreshed by the responses of love and devotion. Mild and loving as a husband and father, yet always firm for the right at the home altar; kind, cheerful, and genial as a companion, a friend, a neighbor, the large-hearted benevolence written upon his face found constant play in the more social relations of life.

As a pastor he was impartial, sympathetic, and tender in all required ministries; as a preacher he was always instructive, often very earnest, and sometimes he brought a magnetic influence to bear upon the attentive hearer; as a reasoner he was methodical rather than incisive, and sought more to persuade than to compel men to believe; as a teacher he was winsome and helpful in developing truth rather than imperious and positive in stating it. In form, of medium height, with broad shoulders and full chest; a ruddy face, susceptible of varied expression; a mild eye that often kindled with feeling, and a physique noticeable for its symmetry, Dr. Tyler stood among the noble Christian workers of his day, the embodiment of qualities and powers of a very high order. His life-work developed in happy proportions practical theology working through practical religion for the salvation of men.

Dr. Tyler was born July 10, 1783, in Middlebury, Conn. At the age of seventeen he entered Yale College, and was graduated in 1804. He studied theology with the Rev. Asahel Hooker of Goshen, was licensed by the Litchfield North Association in 1806, and was installed pastor of the church in South Britain, June, 1808. In 1822 he was elected and made president of Dartmouth College. In 1828 the Second Church in Portland, Me., invited him to become their pastor, and he accepted the call. When this institution was founded in 1834, he was persuaded to give it his services, and continued at the head of it until 1857, when he resigned. His work was nearly done. He died May 14, 1858. The manner of his death is thus recorded: " On the morning of Friday, May 14, 1858, he had taken his usual exercise in the garden of his daughter, Mrs. Greeley, and at nine o'clock entered the house, saying, 'I have finished the garden, if I do not live to eat of its fruit.' He was immediately seized with a neuralgic affection in the head and lungs, from which he suffered exceedingly. He could not be moved home. His wife, children, and grand-children gathered round the bed of the dying patriarch, and received his parting counsels. He was asked if it was a pleasant thought that he should be free from sin. He replied, 'It is the pleasantest thought I have;' then added, with characteristic self-distrust, 'But O, if I should be deceived!' He said little about his feelings: 'I am a great sinner, but Christ is a great Saviour.' 'I have not the ravishing views which some have had, but I enjoy perfect peace.' 'The heart is very deceitful, but I trust I am not deceived; I have no fear.' At eight o'clock in the evening he fell asleep in Jesus."

Monograph on Dr. Nettleton.

ASAHEL NETTLETON was born in North Killingworth, Conn., April 21, 1783, of humble parents. His father, a farmer in moderate circumstances, was esteemed and respected by his neighbors. Both parents were professors of religion, on the Half-way Covenant plan (*i. e.*, on their assent to the covenant of the church—though not admitted to the Lord's table—they were permitted to present their child for baptism.) There had been for half a century a great religious dearth in New England. But now the Spirit of the Lord was poured out in a copious manner. In connection with a published account of the awakening in North Killingworth, the cases of two or three converts, as described by themselves, were printed, and Nettleton was one of them. " It was about ten months from the time when Mr. Nettleton's attention was first seriously turned to the subject of religion before he obtained peace in believing. With him, what the old divines termed the '*law work*,' was deep and thorough. This protracted season of conviction gave him a knowledge of the human heart which few possess, and which was doubtless intended by God to prepare him for that preëminent success which attended his labors as a minister of Christ." In the year 1801 the father of Mr. Nettleton died, and as he was the oldest son the care of the family devolved on him. While expecting to spend his days on the farm his mind was actively reflecting upon the condition of lost sinners in the world. When at work in the field, he would often say to himself, " If I might be the means of saving one soul, I should prefer it to all the riches and honors of this world." He would frequently look forward to eternity, and put to himself the question, "What shall I wish I had done, thousands and millions of years hence?" Samuel J. Mills and Asahel Nettleton were born on the same day. It is a remarkable fact, that their *new birth* occurred very nearly at the same time, that their convictions were similar, and from the commencement their consecration of the same peculiar cast. Nettleton resolved, under the strong pressure of these convictions, to seek an education. While laboring on the farm, he devoted leisure moments to study, reciting occasionally to his pastor, in the winter teaching school, and employing his evenings on studies preparatory to the college course. Thus, in two or three years, he accomplished his plan, and entered the Freshman class of Yale College, in 1805. At that time he was the only professor of religion in his class. In the winter of 1807-8, a revival of religion began in New Haven and Yale College. He was most active and helpful, and especially sought for by those under conviction, for his experience and wise counsels. *He believed*, that *sinners*, properly speaking, never use, but always abuse the means of grace—that in all their efforts to escape future misery and secure future happiness, they are influenced by unholy motives, and that their services are mercenary and sinful. In this opinion, which to him appeared to be clearly taught in the Scripture, he was greatly confirmed by his own religious experience. While under conviction of sin, he had such discoveries of his own heart as to impress indelibly upon his mind a conviction of the entire sinfulness of the religious services of unrenewed men. There was no one point in theology on which his mind was more fully established than this; or one on which he more strenuously insisted during his life, both in the pulpit, and in his conversation with awakened sinners. He considered it a point of great practical importance, and particularly useful in destroying the self-righteous hopes of sinners, and in showing them their lost condition, and entire dependence on the grace of God. This was a weapon which he wielded with great power, and which seemed, in his hands, preëminently "the sword of the Spirit."

I have quoted somewhat at length, this statement of his early and established foundation in the truth, because it is the key, not only to his wonderful mission during the ensuing twenty-five years, but the main ground upon which he became so strenuous and active and successful in laying the foundations of this School of the Prophets fifty years ago.

During the junior year in Yale College, Nettleton became acquainted with Samuel J. Mills, who had come to New Haven for an interview with him, having heard from a mutual friend that "he intended never to be settled, but to be a missionary to the heathen." They compared views and consulted together concerning their future work in Foreign Missions. They "entered into an agreement to avoid all entangling alliances, and to hold themselves in readiness to go to the heathen, whenever God, in his providence, should prepare the way. They also formed the purpose of meeting the next year at Andover, and while pursuing their theological studies, to mature their plans of future action. This purpose, Mr. Nettleton found himself under the painful necessity of abandoning, on account of a debt which he had contracted, while obtaining his education; and which he wished to discharge as soon as possible. He felt the disappointment deeply. Soon after graduation he accepted the office of butler in College, held it for a year, and devoted what leisure time he could command to theological studies. After that he put himself under the instructions of Rev. Bezaleel Pinneo of Milford, with whom he remained until licensed to preach, by New Haven West Association, May 28, 1811.

It is well known that in 1810, Messrs. Judson, Nott, Mills, and Newell, at that time members of Andover Seminary, presented themselves before the General Association of Mass. in Bradford, and made known their convictions of the duty and importance of personally attempting a mission to the heathen, and requested the advice of the Association, and that this movement led to the formation of the American Board of Commissioners for Foreign Missions. Had Mr. Nettleton fulfilled his plan of going to Andover, doubtless he would have been one of that company. When he heard what had been done, he lamented with tears that he could not have been there. He feared that Providence thus indicated that he should not enter the foreign field. He still, however, cherished the purpose, and did not abandon wholly the hope, till the failure of his health in 1822. After his license to preach, on account of the above intention, he declined to be a candidate for settlement in the ministry, and commenced his labors in some waste places and desolate parts of the Lord's vineyard. His labors were crowned with signal success. Wherever he went the Spirit of God seemed to accompany his preaching. His brethren in the ministry, seeing these extraordinary results, advised him to delay his purpose of leaving the country. Acceding to this advice, it became increasingly apparent, that a great work was needed in the churches at home, and that his labors as evangelist were especially owned of God. Accordingly he was ordained as an evangelist in the summer of 1817, by the South Association of Litchfield County.

"In the year 1820, the General Association of Connecticut appointed a committee to take into consideration the subject of increasing ministerial labor in the several congregations of their body. They invited Mr. Nettleton to meet with them, and requested his opinion as to the expediency of introducing and supporting an order of Evangelists. He gave it, as his opinion, that it would be inexpedient to introduce and support such an order. He foresaw the evils that would be likely to grow out of the system, if it were made permanent, and they were the very evils which afterwards arose in some parts of the country, extending their baleful influence to the present time.

From 1812 to 1822 Mr. Nettleton labored in revivals in different parts of this State and often in waste places, with great power from on high, and with the result of the conversion of many precious souls. An account of his work written in 1817, says, "The doctrines taught are those considered as the grand leading truths of the Gospel, viz.: the strict spirituality of the moral law—the total depravity of the natural heart—its enmity to God—the necessity of regeneration by the Holy Spirit—an entire dependence on the merits of Jesus

Christ, for justification, pardon, and acceptance—our obligations to own Him before men, and to manifest our faith in Him by a holy walk and conversation—the divine sovereignty—the electing love of God—and the final perseverance of the saints, as the only ground of the sinner's hope, and the anchor for the Christian's soul."

Mr. Nettleton was not the originator of the measures resulting in the formation of the Pastoral Union of Conn., and the establishment of this Theological Institute; but he was in most hearty sympathy with the purpose of the founders, and took a deep interest in the doctrines declared as the basis of agreement. At the organization he was appointed Professor of Pastoral Duty, but chose not to sustain any official relation to the Institute that he might with the more freedom and effect plead its cause. It may be well to note at this point the esteem in which he was held by the churches, and some of the ablest representatives of the Congregational clergy of New England. When, in 1828, slanderous reports were circulated about him in Virginia, where he was laboring, on account of his faithfulness and convincing power in preaching, testimonials vouching for his character, and attesting the copious abundance of heavenly blessings upon his public ministrations, were forwarded to the Rev. Dr. John H. Rice of that State, signed by the late Dr. Bacon of New Haven, Pres. Day, Profs. Taylor, Goodrich, and Fitch of Yale College. In the year before, Dr. Lyman Beecher, then of Boston, in a letter to the editor of the *Christian Spectator*, says: "Mr. Nettleton has served God and his generation with more self-denial, and wisdom, and success, than any man living. I witnessed his commencement and know his progress, and the relative state of things in Connecticut especially, and what (but for his influence in promoting revivals, and exciting, and teaching by example, others to promote them) might have been the condition of the churches in those days of revolution through which they have passed? And considering how far his knowledge and influence have extended, I regard him as beyond comparison, the greatest benefactor which God has given to this nation. Now that such a man as he should be traduced, and exposed to all manner of evil falsely, is what neither my reason nor my conscience, nor my heart will endure. And in anticipation of the attack which may be, and probably will be made on him, though I am pressed immeasurably with the warfare here, yet sure I am of this, that so long as God spares my life and powers, there is one man certainly, in New England (I know there are thousands) who will consider that in defending him, he defends the cause in one of its most vital points. While I live I am pledged to brother Nettleton by affection, and gratitude, and duty, and nothing could grieve or alarm me more, than to witness in New England, any flinching, or any temporizing in respect to him." Thus spake Lyman Beecher in Boston, when in his prime, he stood up against the encroachments and speculations—then practically taking form—in this suppressed hostility to Mr. Nettleton, and afterwards formulated into a system philosophically undermining the doctrines of grace.

His views on some points of theology, that were spoken without "bated breath" in the year 1834, are briefly touched in some of his letters at that time. Speaking of a certain class of divines he says: "They admit that there is a tendency, or propensity to sin, in the very constitution of the human mind," but they deny that this tendency is sinful. They also admit that "every effect must have a cause, and that this cause must be prior to the effect." Now I observe that the objections which they allege against the views of their opponents, lie equally against their own. It will be no easier for the sinner to repent and believe against this propensity to sin, than it was while it was called a "sinful propensity." Changing the name of a lion into that of a lamb, will not alter its nature. We have here the new philosophy, that all trees are by nature alike, neither good nor bad, until they bear fruit. And then the tree is not good, but the tree is good only *because* the fruit is good, and *vice versa*. "Make the tree good and the fruit will be good," said our Saviour, "for the tree is known by the fruit." "Make the fruit good, and the fruit will be good," says the new philosophy, "for the fruit is known by the fruit. Nothing is good or bad but the fruit. There can be nothing in the tree *itself* back of the fruit, but what is common to all trees—'*pura naturalia.*'"

"On the whole, their views of depravity, of regeneration, and of the mode of preaching to sinners, I think cannot fail of doing very great mischief. This exhibition overlooks the most alarming feature of human depravity, and the very essence of experimental religion. It is directly adapted to prevent sinners from coming under conviction of sin, and to make them think well of themselves, while in an unregenerate state. It flatters others with the delusion that they may give, or have given their hearts to God, while their propensity to sin remains in all its strength. Entertaining this delusion they cannot be converted. Every sinner under deep conviction of sin, knows this statement to be false, so far as his own experience is concerned." "Those who adopt the view I am considering, exhort the sinner to do that only which leaves his propensity to sin in all its strength. Hence conversions are made as easy as you can turn your hand. It is only to resolve and the work is done." This Seminary was founded, as a protest against these views, and to teach a Biblical theology. The writer of this paper can attest the truth of Dr. Nettleton's statement above quoted, from practical experience of that mode of preaching. The instruction was clear and plain, and even when instinctively refused by a rightly-trained conscience, yet made the very impression above asserted. The practical address was: "Young men, you wish to be Christains—go read your Bibles, go and pray, go and do the duty of a Christian, and my word for it, you are a Christian." Some, alas, many it is to be feared, from the present state of the churches, have thus entered into the house of God on earth, while knowing nothing of their own hearts, and still less of Christ as their sacrificial substitute before God for everything. The impression then received was one of satisfaction, in thinking that any time I chose, I could come to that resolution, and then the Spirit of God would put forth His saving influence. As Dr. Nettleton says in another letter, I was taught that "every step in the progress of conviction and conversion, is in direct opposition to these sentiments." The men who advanced these new views, and as they thought important improvements in theology, were brethren beloved, for whom he felt a tender regard, while compelled to dissent from their philosophical speculations, on what he held as the most vital point of Scripture truth.

A large part of the time during his illness, tho' enduring protracted and severe sufferings, his mind was vigorous and active. His resignation and patience were marvelous. The Bible was the man of his counsel. It had been his study for forty years. His Greek Testament and Concordance, were by him daily, for critical study—as the Apostle says he was "expounding spiritual things by the words of the Spirit." He often stayed at my father's house when I was young, and his presence was like the sun for general warmth and blessing. I remember one morning, as I sat gazing on his benevolent face, which seemed to light up, as with some peculiar radiance, he turned and smiling sweetly, called me by name, and said "God commandeth all men, every where now to repent." There was no entreaty, no explanation, but with the words, came a look, a meaning, a power, that have not left my conscience to this day. It was one of the very first indelible impressions on my memory.

His happy way of impressing truth, would be most valuable in this day of open scoffers and latent skepticism, or perhaps one should say "mental reservation" as that is the way many creeds are digested. Meeting a Universalist who wished to discuss "future punishment," he kindly asked him to state his views, so that he could think them over. The man accordingly said, in his opinion, all received their punishment in this life, and would be happy after death. Dr. N. asked him to explain certain Scriptures, as Matt. 25th and others, referring to future judgment, and suggesting to him difficulties for him to solve, without calling in question any of his positions. He then asked him if he believed the account of the Deluge and of the destruction of Sodom and Gomorrah, given by Moses in the Scriptures. "Certainly," he replied. "It seems then," said Dr. N., "that the world was very corrupt, and God determined to destroy it by a deluge. He sent Noah to warn the people. They would not believe him, and the flood came, notwithstanding their unbelief, and, if your theory be true, swept them all up to Heaven. And what became of Noah, that faithful servant of God? He was tossed to and fro on the waters, and was doomed to trials and suffering for three hundred and fifty years longer in this evil world; whereas, if he had been wicked enough, he might have gone up to Heaven with the rest. So with the cities of the plain." After making this statement, he requested the man to reflect on these things, and bade him adieu. A Restorationist once attacked him, and quoted the words from the First Epistle of Peter, to support the doctrine, "By which, He also went and preached to the spirits in prison." Doctor Nettleton observed to him that the time was specified in the next verse, when Christ preached to these spirits in prison. It was "when once the long suffering of God waited in the days of Noah." It was by the Spirit which dwelt in Noah, that he preached to those who are now spirits in prison. "No," said the man, "that cannot be the meaning of the passage. The meaning is, that Christ, after His crucifixion, went down to hell, and preached to the spirits in prison." "Be it so," said Dr. Nettleton, "what did He preach?" "I do not know," he replied, "but I suppose He preached the Gospel." "Do you think," said Dr. Nettleton, "that He preached to them anything different from what He preached on earth?" "Certainly not," said he. "Well," said Dr. Nettleton, "when Christ was on earth, He told sinners that if they should be cast into prison they should not come out thence till they had paid the uttermost farthing. If He went down to hell to preach to the lost spirits there, He doubtless told them 'You must remain here till you have suffered all that your sins deserve.' What influence then would His preaching have, towards releasing them from the place of torment?" Dr. Nettleton thus had amazing power, through his intimate knowledge of the human heart in its enmity against God, and his intimate acquaintance with the Person of God, revealed through Christ in the Scriptures.

Thus led by the Spirit of God, the graces of the Spirit were abundantly manifested in him. His humility was conspicuous. A friend who knew him intimately says: "He was remarkably free from the love of applause. When any one spoke to him of the good he was doing he would sometimes reply, 'We have no time to talk about that,' and frequently I have known him to turn pale and retire from the company, and prostrate himself before God as a great and unworthy sinner."

His meekness was manifest to all who knew him. He bore afflictions of various kinds, the most from those who were enemies of Christ, and who were exasperated by the force and pungency of his preaching. For such he prayed earnestly, and not a few were brought hopefully to repentance and became his ardent friends. His great love for the cardinal doctrines of grace led him to take the deepest interest in this Seminary. Its establishment is largely owing to the seed sown by this man of God, in the country congregations of this State, and his intimate relations with faithful ministers for many years previous to its organization.

We cannot better close this imperfect sketch of the great evangelist, so honored of God in New England, and to whom this Institute is so much indebted, than by quoting his advice to a student of theology. Writing to a student he speaks of the theme he knew the best, and "tho' dead, he yet speaketh," and his words of wisdom may profit us all. "What is the best mode of dealing with anxious souls? Much may be said and written to profit, but after all we might as well ask and answer the question 'What is the best method of treating all manner of sicknesses, and all manner of diseases among the people?' We may talk about the best means of doing good, but after all, the greatest difficulty lies in doing it with a proper spirit. *Speaking the truth in love. In meekness instructing those that oppose themselves. With the meekness and gentleness of Christ.*" In this spirit he lived and wrought, greatly honored of God. His work ended with his life, the 16th May, 1844. But his influence and power, wrought into other lives by the Spirit of God, still are felt in the churches of Connecticut, New York, Massachusetts, and Virginia, where he helped to gather in the spiritual harvests.

In reviewing the life of this wonderful man of God, we have been impressed with the importance and results of his mission among the churches, in its relation to the great work of *Foreign Missions*. Under the Spirit of God, his work here for the production of a new type of Christian character seems to have been as essential for sustaining missions abroad, as the heroic consecration and extraordinary faith of the pioneers themselves.

We have traced, in a desultory way, his aptness for the work of educating and training young converts,—his deep and thorough knowledge of Biblical theology,— his connection with the beginnings of this Seminary,—the proof of his wisdom and foresight,—in the results seen to-day, of the speculations then advanced, as needed by the greater enlightenment of the age ;—his thorough conviction, at the end of life, of the truth of the principles he had maintained from the Word. In all this life-work, his personal bearing and grace fitly illustrated the true spirit of the Gospel—in his interest for, and friendly advice, to students,—his charity and urbanity with opponents,—his gifts and power for personal application of the truth to the individual conscience, as well as his supernatural power in the use of the Word upon public assemblies.

The battle for truth revealed, supernatural, and divine, is commencing again, on virtually the same old grounds of the past, but with a change in the disposition of the forces, and an advance of lines upon the very citadel of God, intimating the nearness of a great crisis! The progress of illumination to-day assails the inspiration of the Holy Scriptures, and practically reduces it to the judgment of the human will. A half-century since the human will only claimed power to regenerate itself. Now it sits in judgment on the Word of God. One lesson of this illustrious life is, that we must maintain the absolute authority of the objective revelation of God, through his Son, in the Holy Scriptures, and to that end, the *plenary verbal inspiration* of the Scriptures, in *every word and letter of the original text.* Especially from the testimonies seen in this life, we are bound to maintain the full and efficacious office of the *Holy Spirit* now to reveal the definite provisions of the atonement of Christ, in their vicarious application to sinners as essential to any *integrity*, in the preaching of the Gospel. And unless *sin* is what God says it is, in its infinite *guilt* and *demerit*, and deserving of what He declares it deserves, in its *unending purpose* and final *restraint*, we have no use for any Bible, and this *man*, and all the ancient *heroes* of *faith*, as well as our Blessed Lord Himself, have lived and died in vain!

The Biblical Teaching of the Seminary, Its distinctive Feature.

It is not a new thing for a theological seminary to claim to be Biblical in its teaching. Indeed, it is to be hoped that it will be many a day before any institution of the kind will not claim to be Biblical. But it requires scarcely a single glance backward in history to discover that much instruction which was once called Biblical would not now be accepted as such. What we rejoice over on this glad occasion, is the fact that this institution, in its genesis and its exodus, as well as in its present land of promise, has rested, and does rest upon the Word of God. The Bible here is not so much a problem as a fact; or better still, perhaps, an aggregation of facts. The efforts of this Seminary are not mainly expended in discussing whether, on the whole, the Bible would better be accepted or not; or what eliminations the closing nineteenth century demands. While affording the fullest opportunity for clearing the atmosphere around such inquiries, it is no part of the purpose of this institution to take anything like the attitude of dictation regarding the divine revelation, or to sit in judgment upon the Word of God, as if that were incomplete without its approval. Hence the influence of the instruction here is not to impress the pupil that the Bible is beclouded with a mist of uncertainty, which it is his mission to explain away.

Trite as this may appear, is it not a point to be emphasized? Is it not a self-evident proposition that, given a Christian theological seminary, there is an accepted revelation from God as the reason for the existence of that institution? And yet it is something, is it not, for the Christian public to be assured beyond a doubt that a theological seminary holds, and impresses upon the minds of its students, strong convictions that the Bible Is?

What is meant, then, when we point to Biblical teaching as the distinctive feature of our beloved institution, may be found in three questions which indicate the character of study and research in each department, viz.: "Has God spoken to men? Has he so spoken that his utterances can be known with certainty?" And last, "What has he said?" Around these three questions the entire system of instruction here may be found, as the radii of a circle spring from its single center and touch the circumference in every direction, however distant. Just here, perhaps, lies one point of its distinction. The aim is not simply to give the student a seminary cast, but to so direct his study of the Bible that he shall receive his moulding influence from the Word of God.

In these halls it is not considered necessary to spend so large a portion of the student's time over the first question of this trio, or even the second; but it is the conviction of this Seminary that, without controversy, and with proof as manifest as it is manifold, God has spoken to man, and in such a way that we may know what his utterances are. Beginning with such a conviction, and holding it with unflinching steadfastness, the main purpose of the teaching of this institution may be said to be not so much to instruct young men in a slavish knowledge of what God has said; and so to send them forth to repeat, parrot-like, what they have already heard,—for it is not intended that the graduate of this Seminary shall go out into the world merely to sprinkle in convenient places the few drops he may have received from a theological hydrant; but the grand intent, and we can conceive of no higher aim, is to teach the student how to find out for himself what the Word of God is. It is not to persuade him of what has been held or said on a few controversial points,—not to take him over solitary passages which have been the historic battlefields of theology; but to so equip him that he can be at home in all parts of Scripture, and at every point. It is desired here, we may affirm, to send out the graduates into the warfare against error, and for truth, not bearing simply a single sword, but being in themselves well-furnished arsenals ready for the use of the Holy Spirit.

Such an aim as this makes the seminary preëminently a place for work. It converts the class and lecture-room into a workshop. It requires the personal contact of the instructor with his pupil. The student must not only be a listener, but a worker; he has not merely the opportunity to hear and know what Bible scholars think and hold, but, if it is in him, he can scarcely fail of becoming, in some useful degree, a Bible scholar himself. This purpose is in perfect keeping with what was once said to the officers and friends of this institution in an inaugural address, and what every student has found true doubtless, in each department, viz., that Biblical teaching here, means preparing young men in the ministry to study the Bible after the strictly scientific method. That is, the discovery, and orderly, accurate arrangement of facts,—facts historical, facts ethical, and facts spiritual, with the triune God as their authority.

It means such deductions, and only such as are clearly based upon this scientific investigation. It means conclusions which are not merely concerning the Bible, or like the Bible, or in possible harmony with the Word of God, but *conclusions which are God's Word.*

Hence it is but just to claim that Biblical teaching here means a conviction that God gave his message to man in human language,—language in use, and subject to the modifications and limitations of the peoples to which it was first spoken. It means that the first, best, and only correct step in learning what God has declared to be his will, is to definitely ascertain the law of the language, the history of the times, and the circumstances of the manifestation in which the Word was given. Then when such steps have been carefully taken, it is considered no discredit to label conclusions so obtained,

DOCTRINES.

It is strength, not weakness, that facts thus established should naturally arrange themselves in harmonious order, and that Biblical teaching in this Seminary should mean a system of divine truth which is at once scientific and authoritative.

Again, it follows as a legitimate and natural result of this method that Biblical teaching, in this center of Biblical study, also means

CANDOR.

On the one hand, the past is not worshiped, as if no more light were to "break forth from the Word of God;" on the other, the past is not discarded, as if no light had broken forth already. The consecrated labors of former years and centuries, are welcomed as making vastly more valuable the discoveries of the present. Here are sought the true of all times. The results here reached are intended to be the sum of the best of the ages, that we may the more accurately come to the knowledge of the exact Word of God.

Further, Biblical teaching carried on in this spirit of candor means

DEVOUTNESS.

Such a method of careful scientific study naturally leads to the stimulation of the devotional nature. For the nearer we get to an adequate, faithful understanding of the human side of God's revelation, the more we are kindled by the divine. The grammar, the lexicon, and the hard work of detail, such as every scholar in these halls is expected to perform, are true factors in spiritual illumination. The student who is conscious that he is able to ascertain what God has said, has an inspiration in that very fact; he feels no need of substituting his wits for Scripture. Indeed, the nearer he gets to what God has declared, the less his own wisdom seems adequate to take its place,—the less inclined will he be to ascribe either value or authority to his own speculations.

Beyond this, we can rightfully claim that Biblical teaching, conducted here after scientific method, with a candid temper, and in a devout spirit, can scarcely become less than Biblical

AUTHORITY.

The real power of the preacher lies, in no small measure, in the Word spoken with conscious authority. But whence comes authority so much as from contact with the Author? It has been truly said that meeting Christ in the Divine

Word, the student is made conscious of the authority of the message he bears. This gives him power. Is the present need of the pulpit, toward the filling of which this Seminary is endeavoring to do its part, greater in any direction, than that it shall be occupied by men who carry with their word the conviction that they are speaking what God has bidden them utter? If there is any confusion in the assemblies of the Lord's house, has it not often arisen because those who stand before the people have shown themselves to be uncertain of their authority? The soul of man is something which will not be bound by any authority less than that of God; so that the real power of preaching is in proportion to the conviction it carries of the authority of God behind it. It is when men hear a voice saying: "Thus saith the Lord, thou art the man;" when they see the finger that points to them, to be the finger of God, and when they forget the man and feel the presence of the Almighty, it is then, and only then we may be sure, that work of eternal value will be done.

It is for this cause that we congratulate ourselves to-day. The Biblical teaching here, puts the student into such close contact with the very Word of God, without the intervention, or discoloration of philosophical spectacles, that he must of necessity feel the life in it, and be himself infused by it. Thus equipped, he goes forth to his life work to give no uncertain sound concerning the truth God hath sent to the children of men.

We are confident that Biblical teaching, as thus imperfectly outlined, is the distinctive feature of this Seminary, not only because we see it to be so, but this also is the impression made wherever its work is felt. In speaking of the graduates of this institution, one of the honored fathers of Connecticut, whose wide experience and observation give no little weight to his testimony, said this of their examinations before installing councils: "These men seem to believe something; they know what it is, why it is, and how to defend it." Not long since, also, a professor in this Seminary, was called to occupy for a Sabbath, a pulpit in a prominent New England city. The day after, a deacon of the church, who was a leading business man, was asked how the preaching of the Hartford representative impressed him. Quick as thought he replied: "Well, one thing is certain, they don't have any fooling down there."

There is weighty testimony, if not elegance, in that reply. It shows, as does the witness from the church councils, that the Gospel as found by the devout, scientific method of Biblical teaching in this institution, is no uncertain sound, but that it is solid, authoritative, and convincing.

It is something to be noted also, in this anniversary, that this Biblical teaching never was more a distinctive feature of the Seminary than at present.

If it is true that these closing years of the fifty which this institution has had of life and labor, have been marked by disturbance in the ebb and flow of the theological tides, it is still a fact that our own alma mater has remained true, with increasing loyalty, to the authority, and adequacy of the Word of God as we have it. If in any quarter, the hold upon the Bible has appeared to be loosening, her grasp has seemed to be the firmer. Truly, she has been like that house upon which the rain descended, and against which floods came and winds blew, but "it fell not for it was founded upon a rock." She too, in her present character, and influence, and in her honorable constituency as well, is a potent example of the enduring, and ennobling nature of the truth to which she holds fast.

But even though it is an anniversary that we this day celebrate, our faces are not backward, but forward. Looking into those years which are just before us,—nearest now, but which will be farthest away from those who shall observe the centennial year, when most of us shall have laid down our armor, —looking into these nearer years, who — what alumni have greater reason for joyful confidence than we, in the future of our Seminary? Our expectancy is not the flush of a new experiment. We are not here to hoist the banner of a new system, uncertain at its very best. But we rejoice in the belief that the prosperity, and the usefulness of this institution are assured as long as it is the business here not merely to furnish men with a few nuggets of gold for distribution, but to equip them with such implements, and to give them such knowledge of their use, as will make them independent, successful miners in the galleries of God's spoken revelation. Such men will not have much time or taste for a noisy proclamation of their own "views," they will be so busy, and so earnest in telling,

"The old, old story that men have loved so long."

While we see, in the Biblical teaching of this Seminary, an element of its safety and its growth, it is not for us, above all men, to forget the utterances of God himself on this matter: "The grass withereth, the flower fadeth, but the Word of our God shall stand forever." "Heaven and earth shall pass away, but my Word shall not pass away." They stand longest and surest who stand nearest to the Word.

So of the glory of this institution; it is not worth while to ask any other than that which comes from the same source.

Some of us will not soon forget a remark made by one of the instructors here in the days when the classes were smaller than at this date. Referring to the increase of students, he said: "Young men, what we must seek in this Seminary is quality not quantity." This is the true watch-word for the alumni in desiring the glory of our beloved school of the prophets; it is quality rather than size. It is the glory of the reflected light of the Word of God. As long as Biblical teaching shall thus be the distinctive feature of this institution, just so long will the glory of God in the Holy Spirit overshadow the character and the work of those who come and go, in and out of the Hartford Theological Seminary.

The Theological Seminary and Foreign Missions.

The origin of foreign missions in New England was contemporary with that of theological seminaries. The first known instance within the present century of personal consecration to the foreign service was by an undergraduate at Williams College, the same year that Andover Seminary was founded; while the first class from that Seminary graduated the same year with the organization of the American Board. It will always remain a suggestive incident that Mr. John Norris of Salem, being deeply impressed with the claims of missions, and often uttering the sentiment, "The missionary object is the greatest in the world!" was at first disposed to give only five thousand dollars toward an endowment at Andover; but on the suggestion of his wife, that the two objects are the same, he made the amount ten thousand dollars. Later, his widow bequeathed thirty thousand to the Seminary, and an equal sum in aid of missions to the heathen.

Among the fathers, founders, and early officers of the institution whose semi-centenary we celebrate to-day, there was not wanting a regard to the interests of foreign evangelism. They were men neither of narrow minds nor of shriveled sympathies. Among them were those who had weighed seriously the duty of going in person to the heathen; who prayed for the universal spread of the Gospel, whose contributions to that object were not small, though they made large sacrifices for the new Seminary. One of them gave a son to Africa, where he has already spent thirty-five years of Christian service among the Zulus. We might expect that such a spirit would impart character, in some good measure, to the sentiment of successive classes of students. Recent correspondence with living alumni who have been, or are now in foreign fields, bears testimony that the monthly concert of prayer was maintained here with interest; that the missionary meetings of Tuesday evening were far the best; that seldom did a student absent himself; that a union of those contemplating foreign work was early formed, and that love for missions was sustained by the personal interest of the Professors. "I spent but one year—my senior year—in Hartford Seminary," writes a graduate, "but it is a year full of blessed memories, because it brought me nearer to Christ; gave me an intense longing to know and do only his will; to seek souls, not place; to labor anywhere and in any way that might best promote the glory of Him who redeemed us with his most precious blood. Willingness to labor as a foreign missionary became in Hartford Seminary a decision to do so, if God should open the way."

An alumnus who has for ten years had charge of a mission theological seminary, expresses the conviction, in a letter just received, that all candidates for the ministry, including those for foreign service, should become familiarized with the principles and leading methods of evangelistic work abroad as well as at home, not that a training-school for missionaries should be established, but that in the lecture-rooms of existing institutions there should be instruction beyond what is generally given at present. This falls in with the theme assigned to me—the place of missions in a theological curriculum; and it is a happy circumstance that what I have to say can be said without the least comparative reflection upon the past or the present of Hartford Seminary.

As regards distinct, formal instruction on this subject, what is the condition of things in training-schools for the ministry throughout our land? The question is not whether interest in missions has been felt, and whether, in the department of church history, more or less of instruction has been given; but the question is, What status has Evangelistic Theology, as a branch by itself? Not till January, 1867, was *permanent* provision made for *distinct* instruction in this line, at any one of our professional schools. The endowment of the Hyde

Lectureship of Foreign Missions in the Andover Seminary, with a fund of five thousand dollars, less than a score of years since, marked an epoch in ministerial training. Nothing could be more appropriate than that the oldest seminary in our country—save, perhaps, that of the Moravians, at Bethlehem, Pennsylvania—the foster mother of so many sons who have entered foreign missionary fields, should take the lead in an an arrangement of this kind. True, fifty years ago the General Assembly of the Presbyterian Church, with a breadth of enterprise quite in advance of that period, instituted a chair at Princeton, with a special, though not exclusive regard to this subject; but it was filled for only a short time. Seven years after the founding of the Lectureship at Andover, the Union Theological Seminary of New York city established a mixed professorship of "pastoral theology, church polity and mission work," and the incumbent lectures twice a week to the junior class, through the first term, on the subject last named. That was the next instance in which this department of ministerial propædeutics found recognition in a permanent organic form.

From a comparative survey of theological institutions in the United States, it would seem that those of the Methodist Episcopal Church come abreast with the most advanced in distinctness of aim as relates to this department. What else might be expected of a denomination in which the missionary idea is, to so commendable a degree, dominant—an idea which enters formally into the very constitution and prescribed administration of the church. The first seminary of that denomination, for theological training, was established at Concord, New Hampshire, in 1847; was twenty years afterwards removed to Boston, and is now the School of Theology connected with the Boston University. In its curriculum is a missionary course; but the elaborate plan has not been carried out, though it only awaits required funds. Yet for thirteen years past, a weekly lecture on some missionary topic has been supplied by one of the Faculty, and special courses are also occasionally delivered by gentlemen from outside. The Drew Theological Seminary at Madison, New

Jersey, announces that it aims to give due prominence to those kinds of instruction which are needed by students proposing to go as missionaries to foreign countries, and by ministers at home. They are referred to the best books on the history of missions, and are required to become particularly familiar with the history, the fields of labor and plans of action of their own missionary society. The subject is presented to them by lectures, with reference to those paragraphs of the church discipline which officially set forth the method of raising and appropriating funds—also to the annual reports of their missionary society. After explanations and sufficient time for consulting the references given, each man is required to be prepared to state exhaustively the whole topic or any part of it, with a view to his being qualified to present the claims of the society to any congregation, so as to secure its intelligent and liberal support.

The inquiry here arises, Where, in the field of institutional studies, a chair of missions may have place—what are its logical relationships? Biblical Theology supplies the starting-point; and among urgent desiderata of the day—one worthy of the highest scholarship—is painstaking, exhaustive exegesis, together with inferential exposition of all Scriptures relating to the nature and compass of the Messianic Kingdom; to the character, condition, and destiny of the unevangelized; to the universal need and universal adaptation of Christianity, and to its predicted triumphs.

Thence we would pass to the department of Practical Theology, and gather into systematic form, the teachings of our Lord and His Apostles, regarding the bounden aggressiveness of Christianity; the proper motives for evangelizing the heathen; the need of general consecration to the work; the power and need of prayer specifically for the coming of the Kingdom. The principles, forms, and proceedings of home organizations; the policies and methods of missions abroad, with a multitude of topics, will engage the instructor's attention. In both Biblical Theology and Biblical Ethics there would be left a domain too broad ever to be exhausted by their respective professors.

Then comes the obvious element which gives this subject a place in church history. There is certainly required a glance at primative gospel promulgation, including the causes and consequences of decline in evangelistic zeal; mediæval missions; modern Roman Catholic propagandism; tentative Protestant efforts in the seventeenth century; the rise of organized evangelism among heathen nations at the beginning of the last century; the signal growth thereof at the close of that century and thence onward to the present time. There are now more than eighty foreign missionary societies, each of which has for its object what was the motto of one established in the Netherlands, 1797, " Peace through the blood of the cross," each of which deserves notice, and some of which would require years of study. Portraits of heroes and heroines in the great enterprise would fill a gallery. So would the portraits of eminent converts from heathenism. No small space would be due to trials endured and obstacles encountered; and among the latter might come the comparative study of false religions. Direct results are an ample and animating theme. Indirect results, in benefits accruing to commerce, to geography, ethnography, philology, and natural science, deserve consideration; and still more the reflex influence on churches at home, and the general culture of the community. These are topics but slightly touched upon at the present time in our seminaries, and topics which any professor of Ecclesiastical History would be glad to have treated by some able coadjutor. One attractive feature in this department is that a comparatively virgin soil presents itself, and there exist vast stores of undigested facts to be carefully explored, as well as great problems to be solved.

It must seem plain that there is here a broad field for cultivation, and that it is one for which no adequate specific provision has been made. Indeed schools of the prophets generally, with all the advances that have taken place, seem not to have kept pace with certain other institutions. There are lines of higher education in the United States which, during the fifty years that measure the life of this Seminary, furnish suggestive lessons. Look at schools of science, of which

West Point, Annapolis, the Sheffield, and Lawrence schools were the only ones of importance half a century ago. Now there are colleges of agriculture and the mechanic arts to the number of eighty-five, seventy-two of which have sprung into existence since 1834. But it is not the increase of number so much as the sums devoted to their establishment that surprise and gratify us. Including grounds, buildings and productive funds, those institutions have endowments amounting to twenty-four and a half millions of dollars. Among the branches taught, of which we scarcely heard anything fifty years ago, are physiological chemistry, agricultural chemistry, molecular physics, mathematical physics, biology, dynamic engineering, and so on through a long catalogue. These schools of technology or applied science, have grown out of the practical demands of the age, and are training men to employ principles wrought out by master spirits in the university, and to put them upon making fingers of steel instead of flesh, to weave and twist; upon constructing machines that shall compel mountains to disgorge their treasures; upon devising apparatus that annihilates distance; and upon manifold applications that subsidize the forces of nature, superseding the artisan, changing methods and times of intercommunication, and thus revolutionizing the ways of commerce. An animating record, but it is eagerness for material prosperity that incites to all this.

Collegiate institutions have made noteworthy advancement. Passing up this valley of the Connecticut fifty years ago, we should have found Amherst College with a president, five professors and four tutors; to-day we find a president, seventeen professors and six additional instructors. New departments of study have been introduced, and the funds of the institution have been increased by a million of dollars. In 1834 Yale College reported a faculty of eight professors, including the president, besides ten other instructors; Yale now reports twenty-three professors, including the president, besides eleven other instructors, and a corresponding increase of funds, buildings, and library belonging to the academical department. At Harvard, half a century ago, there were seventeen teachers in the undergraduate department, besides four lecturers who did no class work ; now there are fifty-four teachers, besides twelve or fifteen more with whom students may take electives. And what an array of courses at the present time—enough to amaze the graduate of 1834 !—eight elective courses in the Semitic languages, including Hebrew, Aramaic, Assyrian, and Arabic ; four in the Indo-Aranian languages, including Sanscrit and the old Iranian; thirteen in Greek; twelve in Latin ; two in Greek and Latin Comparative Philology; nine in the English Language and Literature ; eight each in German and French ; four in Italian; three in Spanish ; eleven in Philosophy ; seven in Political Economy ; seventeen in History ; three in Roman Law ; seven in the Fine Arts ; six in Music ; ten in Mathematics ; eight in Physics ; nine in Chemistry, and eighteen in Natural Philosophy. As for funds, they are now ten times what they were then.

Turn to professional education, and glance for a moment at medical schools. Multiform divisions have been made in the old standard departments of anatomy, surgery, materia medica, theory, and practice. New departments have sprung up, resulting from advance in the science of chemistry, and from new appliances, such as the achromatic microscope, etherization, and the like. It is not, perhaps, beyond the recollection of aged persons, when there were only three teachers at each of our leading medical schools, where there are now from one score to two score professors. In regard to almost every leading branch fifty years ago, Dr. Holmes might well say, " I call it a chair—it was rather a settee of professorships." The medical department of Columbia College in the city of New York, has a faculty at this time numbering fourteen professors, besides twelve clinical professors. The corresponding department in the University of the City of New York, enumerates eighteen or twenty gentlemen on its regular staff, six adjunct lecturers, and laboratory instructors. Harvard University in its medical school, and for its one hundred and first annual announcement (1884), enumerates a faculty with twenty-two members, eighteen other stated instructors, besides eight or more who give special clinical instruction, making a staff of forty-six gentlemen. Will any well-informed person pronounce that number needlessly great—that the costly laboratories, museums, libraries, and other adjuncts, are too expensive in view of the reliefs contemplated for human suffering and anxieties, and the vast sanitary benefits to the community?

In our theological seminaries sub-divisions have indeed taken place, to a noticeable extent, within these fifty years. Biblical philology once embraced Hebrew and Greek; also, it may be Old Testament theology and New Testament theology, not to speak of Assyriology, which, to be sure, has no frequent place as yet. The comprehensive department, earlier known to us as that of dogmatic theology, may now be seen partitioned into professorships of natural theology, apologetics, and also of the relations of science to theology; while the department of church history has been sub-divided into the history of facts and the history of doctrines. Homiletics and elocution are, in some instances, provided for under separate teachers, whereas sacred rhetoric formerly embraced the two. Nor is this all; to the old curriculum there has been added a department of ecclesiastical music and hymnology.

Increased division of labor, and consequent increase in the staff of instructors, suggest, it may be, a liability to excessive crowding, to superficiality, or confusion, if all the diversified fields are to be traversed during a triennium; and hence suggest also whether certain matters which may be considered rather as adjuncts cannot be made elective for a limited number of students who have special aptitudes; or whether such matters should not be reserved for a year supplementary to the three years of urgently needful studies. In case a fourth year were added to the regular course of every such institution, or if a more extended post-graduate course were instituted, with two or three professorships adequately endowed, theological seminaries would still lag behind medical schools in such appointments. The medical department of the University of Pennsylvania now has a post-graduate course, with not less than a dozen departments and as many different professors; the New York Post-graduate School advertises a faculty numbering fourteen professors; and similar provision for advanced study exists elsewhere also. We, of course, rejoice to see the rapid advance of high education in other spheres; but is it creditable to the Church of Christ that she has made no more ample provision for the training of young men devoted to infinitely higher concerns?

It would be superfluous to enlarge here on the high aims and the moral earnestness demanded of the minister of the Word. Eminent duties of leadership devolve upon him. By his very profession he is bound to cherish breadth of view and a breadth of sympathy commensurate with the living race of mankind—an interest so habitual that his thoughts will never, for any length of time, stop short of India, China, or Polynesia. Indeed, he should be a man of one idea, but that idea broad as the world and the reach of eternity. If a home pastor, or home missionary, he needs the inspiration of this grand thought, the ultimate universal sway of Immanuel. Beyond anything else will it prove a mental and moral tonic, rousing from intellectual sluggishness, perfunctory contentment, and-contented poverty of thought. Whatever may be true regarding advanced thought, there certainly is need of advanced discipleship. The home pastorate, be it repeated, requires the expanding influence of this sovereign purpose so in harmony with the sublimest enterprise of all time. What was Baxter's range of thought in his unsurpassed parochial activity and success in reforming irreligious Kidderminster? "There is nothing in the world," he writes, "that lies so heavy upon my heart, as the thought of the miserable nations of the earth. I cannot be affected so much with the calamities of my own relations, or of the land of my nativity, as with the case of the heathen, Mohammedan, ignorant nations of the earth. No part of my prayer is so deeply serious, as that for the infidel and ungodly world." Ministers with minds thus expanded and hearts thus burdened will not aim at merely the spiritual safety of parishioners, but that they may be saved to labor, and that vigorously, in the Master's vineyard; they will seek to train the entire church as a missionary band; effective interest in the work abroad will be reckoned among needful proofs of reputable membership; the multitudes of professing Christians who live in scandalous apathy, or in scandalous waste of wealth, will grow less; patriotism will merge itself in philanthropy, and philanthropy in an unquenchable desire for the conversion of all men. Nor will this be a fitful desire awakened only at great spirited gatherings; the well-equipped pastor will resolutely and steadily keep heart; will maintain faith and love in such a glow as not to require outside help in kindling his own fires.

An eminent Prussian minister of education remarked: "Whatever you would have appear in the life of a nation, you must put into its schools." With no less truth may it be said, whatever we would have in the life of the churches we must put into the theological school. Not that the ideal minister can be made to order; nor that the seminary is immediately responsible for defective training in the family and the Sunday-school; yet a degree of indirect responsibility does exist. Reasonably is it demanded of the professional course that it have a well-directed purpose to supply, not only educated brain, but consecrated hearts—hearts inspired with zeal for advancing the great object of redemption—animated by the certainty of that imperial sway which Jesus Christ is yet to have in this world, and which will be achieved by the preaching of His own glorious Gospel.

It is submitted, therefore, that in such professional seats a larger place should be given to the history, the claims, the principles, the methods, the fruits of this grand enterprise. It is submitted that if the College of Apostles were in consultation on the establishment of a training-school for discipleing all nations, evangelistic theology would be the overshadowing department, and the chair of foreign missions would have no mere by-place. On the one hundredth anniversary of the death of Count Zinzendorf, the founder of Moravian missions, a German writer remarked: "It seems to me to belong to the many contradictions that we meet with in life, that theologians should leave the university with a knowledge of ancient gnosticism, but with none whatever of an institution with which their profession will be sure to bring them often in contact." True indeed, and passing strange it is, that by some of the theological faculties of Germany, everything is taught except the one thing; and we cannot help appreciating the sturdy practical sense of Gossner, a founder of missions who, when the writing-desk of Hegel the philosopher was presented to the hospital, converted it into a kitchen table. No oblique thrust at industry and accuracy of scholarship in any existing department of study is intended. Rather, we say, let there be yet other departments, and a more accomplished scholarship. The broader the culture, and the more ample the furniture, the better is the preparation for simplest work and for narrow spheres. But it is claimed that the universal propagation of the Gospel, as an object of study and interest, should be interwoven among the fibers of every student's heart; that he should not be thought qualified for graduation till he possesses well-defined ideas concerning the greatness and obligations of the work; till he has mastered an outline of its progress hitherto, and of its present activities; till he knows what the best sources of information are, and is at least prepared to build up for himself a symmetrical evangelistic culture. Is it suggested that whole classes might sometimes go abroad? Blessed result! The God of all the earth, and our risen Lord, who is "expecting till his enemies be made his footstool," and who is wondering at the self-indulgent disloyalty of his professed followers, will look after such an institution, and the churches and country that sustain it. Not less than with the individual, will the seminary that shall thus lose its life for Christ's sake and the Gospel's, save it.

But when will our denomination be fired with any such intense evangelistic ardor as an open heathen world and its accessible millions demand? Lectureships and professorships on missions will not, indeed, of themselves supply our own country or the heathen world with the men required. Well has it been said, "A drop of life is better than a sea of knowledge." Yet improved appliances can hardly fail, in some measure, to expand and ennoble that curriculum through which candidates for the sacred office are to pass. We would fain deem it not too bold a prediction that, without retrenchment elsewhere, there will be enlargement in this direction; that by the close of the present century our theological seminaries will be supplied with such an auxiliary, or something tantamount thereto. In that new and mighty baptism of Christian enterprise, which we pray God may be near, it will be demanded that every theological institution become a well-endowed academy of spiritual strategics and energetic Christian warfare.

Sound theology alone will not suffice; orthodoxy in action, in suffering, and sacrifice, is demanded. Calvinism made the French Huguenot and the English Puritan; it has made many a powerful preacher, and many a brave missionary. Holding that there are other ethical elements in the divine character besides love; that the inevitable penalty of sin, unrepented of in this life, is endless punishment; that salvation from sin and from the abiding wrath of God is possible only through the infinite merits of an expiatory sacrifice; it holds also that every living man, woman, and child in Christendom is bound to make utmost efforts to evangelize the nations. This is simply Pauline theology—an incisive Christology, that both broadens and intensifies the inner man. It discerns no heroism in hermits on the top of pillars or in caverns. Duty without compromise, is its motto. Scipio affirmed there was not a man in his army who would not, at the word of command, climb a tower and cast himself into the sea. Is a lower grade of obedience seemly in the sacramental host?

Late correspondence with missionary alumni of this institution discloses gratifying loyalty to the aim, methods, and theological attitude of their *alma mater*. Repeated and grateful reference is made to the eminently Biblical training given here, one result of which is a deepening love for the Sacred Scriptures; to the type of Biblical exegesis, which has enabled these brethren to know where and how to find that truth which they are to preach. Among those brethren there is but one voice in regard to the instruction—that the theology taught has stood them well in all their work; that it is effective and commands respect; that as experience accumulates, greater confidence is felt in the teaching of this Seminary. One of our honored and beloved brethren, writing from Turkey, says—and others say the same substantially—"As I look back over sixteen years of missionary life, I am most thoroughly convinced that the distinctive doctrines which were the basis of all the instructions given there are the only doctrines which will suffice to arouse these nominal Christians for whom we labor, from their fatal trust in outward rites, and bring them up to a life 'hid with Christ in God.' The fearful depravity so rife among all these peoples, whether Christian or Mohammedan—of which the delineations of the first chapter of the Epistle to the Romans are no exaggeration—can only be removed 'by the washing of regeneration and by the renewing of the Holy Ghost.' The people are 'lost,' 'condemned already,' and only the plain, pertinent, presentations of the truths of the Divine Word unmixed with human speculations, can save them."

It is a gratifying circumstance that a larger proportion of students who have been connected with the Hartford Seminary should enter upon missionary work at home or abroad, than from any other of our seven similar institutions, if not a larger proportion than from any similar seminary of whatever denomination in the land. The first graduating class (1836) furnished a missionary to the Sandwich Islands; the second furnished one for the Spokan Indians far to the Northwest; and it illustrates the wonderful progress of things that, whereas forty-five years ago, he found one hundred and twenty-nine days were required for the journey from Westport, Mo., to the place of destination in Washington Territory, only four days were needed for the recent and first return of this hale brother of 74. Others of our number have or have had their frontier posts in Mexico, Austria, Bulgaria, Turkey, Syria, India, China, Micronesia, South and Southwestern Africa.

Some of them have had their share in the translation of God's Word and the production of useful literature in various vernaculars, and all testify to joys and successes in many a dark spot of the heathen world.

Four of the goodly band rest from their labors. One lies buried in the cemetery of Cedar Hill in this city; one had had his watch-tower on Mount Lebanon; Brewster survived only a month after reaching China, and Maynard had but just entered upon his work on the site of ancient Thessalonica. Visiting Mount Olympus and the Vale of Tempe, he contracted a fever which took him to the Mount Zion above. Did ever Grecian hero, philosopher, or poet utter words so full of meaning as that young soldier of the cross in his last sickness—breaking forth into exclamations—" What a glorious Gospel! What a lovely Savior!" Visiting the grave of Maynard you will pass by Thermopylæ. The simple inscription with which Sparta commemorated the heroic devotion of Leonidas and his faithful band was: " Stranger, tell the Lacedemonians that we lie here in obedience to their laws." This is a decoration-day for deceased comrades. We visit tombstones scattered among the hills of New England and broad plains of the West; one amidst the evergreen foliage of the tropics; one beside the monuments of Morrison and Bridgman, and another looking out upon the Ægean. In each hand we carry a wreath. One motto for our fallen brethren is, " We lie here in obedience to our Master's command;" the other, " We are more than conquerors."

The Survival of the Ax.

When the young prophets of the Gilgal band
Their sacred college for Elisha planned,
And sought the waving woods, by Jordan's stream,
To gather timber, "every man a beam,"
They little guessed a miracle would crown
One small mischance with swift and sure renown,
And make the story of their work sublime
In records broad as earth and long as time.
 Behold Elisha and his student train !
Cheerful they march, and soon the woodland gain.
Strong to his pious task each laborer bends ;
In sturdy concert every ax descends,
And musical thro' all the forest shades
Peal the sharp echoes of their ringing blades.
One eager workman hews with hasty blows
A tree whose roots the river overflows.
Sudden his stroke flies wild : a flash, a gleam—
And the loose steel falls splashing in the stream.
Gazing with eyes perplexed he sees it sink ;
With helve in hand he stands upon the brink :
Surprise and fear his startled conscience tax—
"Alas, my master ! 'twas a borrowed ax !"
Then waits with mute appeal, as if to trace
Some hopeful counsel in the prophet's face.
 Calm o'er the water, at his pupil's call,
Elisha looked : "My son, where did it fall ?"
He stretched his hand ; he bade the waves unclose ;
And the sunk iron to the surface rose.
The grateful youth his lost utensil won,
Fixed firm its handle—and the work went on.

 Since that strange scene nine hundred years, and more,
Had passed—and, heard again on Jordan's shore,
Elisha's miracle smote high and low
As if Elisha's master dealt the blow,—

"Fall barren trees, and trees of worthless fruit!
Fall for the fire! the ax is at your root!"
And some who listened seemed to understand,
And cried, convicted, "'Tis Elijah's hand!"
Thro' tangled errors darting quick dismay,
The mighty cleaver cut its fearless way;
Hewed falsehood down, slew folly at its side,
Struck bigotry, and unbelief. and pride,
Bared old abuses, laid rank envies low,
And battered power ungodly, blow on blow,
Till the dark, pathless wilderness of sin
Opened and let the Morning Star shine in.
    It was enough. The ax immortal flew
From the bold hand that wielded it so true,
For hurled at Herod's shame, at last it found
A heart too willing to resent the wound,
And where the smiter-prophet last had stood
Herodias' vengeance left it drowned in blood.
    Drowned, but not perished. Ere the saddening scene
Of cruel triumph passed, that engine keen
Forth on its spoilers' heads like lightning broke,
And Jews and Gentiles trembled at the stroke.
With force fresh-harnessed for the sharp assault,
It rose at ancient wrong in stern revolt,
And hoar hypocrisy drove skulking out,
And moss-grown ignorance, and chronic doubt,
And blind tradition, and inveterate caste
Felt its fierce impact like a whirlwind's blast.
In vain old darkness, strong-surrounding, set
Its prisoners' bondage—light was stronger yet,
And jealous hate might murder righteous John;
The truth survived—and still the work went on.

    O, oft in later time, when, wielded well,
That implement of power on Falsehood fell;
When her tall trees its lightnings earthward hurled,
And the grand strokes went sounding thro' the world,
And o'er the prostrate forms of things abhorred
Made pathway for the coming of the Lord,
Some paltry failure or unseen despite
Has turned its aim,—or whirled it out of sight!
'Tis but the laborer's fortune: Who can pledge
Thro' Error's wilderness the whetted edge,

And always for the task his hope has planned
Be sure the instrument is well in hand?
A human weakness or mistake may foil
Its promised force, and mar the best man's toil.
But, tho' he mourn it as a blessing past,
It will return, and serve him to the last.
   Truth is a tool of trenchant virtue, old,
And plain of pattern, but of strength untold.
Forged of celestial steel, and tempered just,
It cuts unfailing—and it cannot rust.
Only one thing it needs, for service' sake—
Give it a handle of terrestrial make;
And, earthly wood to heavenly metal hung,
You have the ax that John the Baptist swung.
   That ax is never lost; tho' sometimes, when
The wielders of its weight are mighty men,
Who at some evil root too fiercely delve,
It slips its fastening, and flies off the helve.
Wait then, exultant foe and timid friend,
That is its accident, and not its end,
And, save some sad distemper holds them dim,
The eyes that saw it sink will see it swim.
Sure as the light restores the moons that wane,
The sacred blade resumes its haft again;
Its sounding shock the shades of death anon
Confess and fear—and still the work goes on.

   Brethren and reverend fathers! when, aglow
With Christ's pure gospel, fifty years ago,
By old Connecticut's untainted tide,
You stood, in faith resistant, side by side,
To Innovation's overgrown demands,
You held that ax in no unpracticed hands.
Those hands wrought nobly what your hearts had willed;
Those hearts took counsel, " Let us rise and build!
Here, o'er the waters hallowed by the flame
Of Edwards' genius, power, and saintly fame,
A prophets' school shall stand, whose voice shall speak
The old instruction when the church is weak.
Here shall faith's fortress be, for dangerous days
When Israel's sons forget the ancient ways,
To lift the cross of Christ, and guard intent
The word and doctrine of His Testament."

I see them by the old colonial stream,
The builders, gathering every man a beam.
How humble was their work! and yet more grand
Than patriots' warfare for their native land;
And truth within their grasp had nobler sweep
Than conquerors' swords that Honor's harvests reap.
Religion's cause inspired them: 'twas their hour
To add new height to Zion's beacon-tower.
They toiled for man—that mortals need not fear
To miss salvation's pathway, once so clear,
And while with brave and patient hands they mowed
The upstart growths that choked the heavenly road,
Like them who Jordan's oaks by Gilgal slew
They smote to save, and spoiled to make anew.
Error's tall wildings cleft in planks of strength,
And branching mischiefs laid at harmless length,
Experience carved from danger, hope from fear,
And green pretension slain to life sincere,
Opinions tough thro' long polemic storm,
And rank young fancies, pruned alike to form
Eccentric theories tamed in rash increase,
And sprouting hatreds punished into peace,
Warped stems of doctrine straightened on the ground,
Folly's soft saplings hewed to wisdom sound,
Half-truths for use transfixed in swift escape,
Raw notions whittled into safer shape,
Lopped and converted water-shoots of doubt,
False scions cut to bleed their poison out,
And high-grown learning clipped and sanctified,
And sundered trunks of sophistry and pride,
And baffled heresy, and pricked conceit,
And roots of bitterness crushed under feet—
These were their trophies; gracious Providence
Would make faith's perils furnish faith's defence,
And bid her champions bear the spoils they win
Home to their infant walls, and build them in.
Such was th' eternal plan,—that ruined wrong
Should make the towers of righteousness more strong;
That holiest good should spring from evil slain,
And ransomed losses heighten final gain,
And things of blessing grow from things accurst,
And in one race the best replace the worst,
Till Adam's glory quenched in Jesus beamed,
And man once fallen rose to man redeemed.

And so the work went on: those royal few
Each to the burden set his shoulder true,
And soon on massive mound and solid pier,
In strength firm-pinioned, growing, tier on tier,
Went up the walls,—and stately stood, and still,
Faith's edifice on fair East Windsor Hill.
   The prophets had their home; but full reward
Must wait while yet they builded for the Lord.
Nor were their future trials unforeshown
When white-haired Perkins laid the corner-stone:
They saw unmoved their high adventure born
'Mid forests of distrust and envious scorn,
And knew that, win or fail, as heaven should please,
The ax of Truth must strike unyielding trees.
Yet bated not their toil those workmen stern,
Nor spared the edge, to sever and discern,
Where fatal frauds and loose beliefs prevailed,
Nor missed a stroke,—until their money failed.
   Ah, what to pious knight or crusade king
Is heaven-forged weapon, if it will not swing?
Thoughtful they paused. In vain the champion's might
With steel unsocketed in act to smite!
No matter "where it fell," the blade new-drawn
Lay ineffectual with its handle gone,
And hinted duty and remembered text,
That needy hour, their Christian souls perplexed.
"Shall God on man depend, and truth no more
Unfurnished win its way, as when of yore
John and Elijah preached in camel's hair
From a turf pulpit, in the open air?"
And then their musings took a deeper tone,
"The ax was borrowed,—it was not our own.
The heir loom of eternity unpriced,
We had it from the wounded hands of Christ:
Tempered in altar-fires, at countless cost,
What would be said in heaven if it were lost?"
   But soon they faced their trial unappalled,
And timely aid serener thoughts recalled,
For the great Master, whom their hearts adored,
To their miscarried power the stock restored,
And stretching hands of faith, those holy men,
Rejoicing, felt it in their grasp again.
   And ever after, if, by hap or blame
The truth fell sidelong, cheated of its aim,

When Geshems and Tobiahs lurked behind,
And sly Sanballats plotted, sapped, and mined,
When friends were few, and fewer came to fill
The empty halls and chambers on the " Hill,"
Surely and soon the helpless moment passed,
And patience found its arm of strength at last.
" Take courage, men of God, and learn to bless
The same recovery in the same distress.
These are but casual slips : the grand career
Stops not for trifles happening there or here
To warn our wisdom that for weak or strong
Right has its accidents as well as wrong."
 So the brave workmen cheered their hearts—and loved
The more their sacred trust in peril proved,
As each misfortune taught them more to prize
The wondrous weapon lent them from the skies.
It was their miracle. No hard rebuff
Could dull a tool of such celestial stuff,
Nor theft nor burial hide it anywhere
Beyond the summons of their faithful prayer.
And when from their old home's abandoned wall
They dreamed they heard it in the river fall,
And faltering friends, with weak, untimely pride,
Passed by East Windsor on the other side,
So far from ended was its mission then,
It swam to Hartford—and began again.
There for its tireless force the prophets found
Unhindered task on better vantage-ground ;
Their prayers were answered ; all their doubts were gone ;
Hope gave the word—and still the work went on.

 Brethren and fathers ; many a morrow's sun
Must rise and set before your work is done.
When culture, from the heights where science feeds
In " new departure " sends her tinkered creeds,
When Paul's plain text philosophy defines
To suit smart thinkers tired of Gospel lines,
When faith's strait way is broad and broader made,
And skeptics gladden at the easier grade,
And *depth* of grace that means a heart renewed
Is changed for theologic *latitude ;—*
When round the house of God such plants as these
Grow tall, and crowd the grand primeval trees,
Firm at your station duty bids you stand
In full fidelity of heart and hand.

The garden of the church is choked; and here
In your untiring strife to keep it clear
Against the upshoots of anointed sham,
Your tool of strength must be the ax that swam.
Still wield the ancient truth, and, in your hold,
Plied with such vigor, and with zeal as bold
As fired the spirits of the holy Twelve,
The Salem blade with the East Windsor helve
Will cut resistless till its way is won,
And the Voice over Jordan speaks—" Well done;"
And your victorious souls within the vail,
With sainted Tyler, Nettleton, and Yale,
Perkins, and Ely, Dow, Calhoun, and Dodd,
And Hyde, and Spring, and Tenney, rest in God.
   Benignant Tyler! foremost in the band
Whose faith this fort of orthodoxy planned,—
The dew of his sweet influence still is shed
On us who heard the gracious words he said,
And his dear memory to new joy unfolds
Each thankful heart that now his image holds.
His was a noble presence, frank, refined,
To win obeisance from the manliest mind,
While all his balanced powers confirmed and held
Perpetual the respect his mien compelled.
Prophet of God, with Moses' meekness crowned!
Was ever leader wiser, kinder found?
And say, what cloistered doctor could exceed
In piety that Israelite indeed?
He was a man of prayer, profoundly good,
And brave as Samuel by the Ark he stood;
A man of peace, yet strenuous to contend
When speculation dared the truth to bend:
Strong in the Word, one aim his soul engrossed,
To teach the sense that honors God the most,
While faithful, scorning all sophistic play,
He led to heaven by the straightest way.
We have not lost him; still affection's eye
Traces his lengthened pathway to the sky,
And follows far, where up the blue incline
His pure life, passing, left its shining line,
Till his calm face and well-known smile are seen
Among the haloed heads in bliss serene.
The same blest presence to our filial thought
Pervades where long and last he toiled and taught,

Where sympathies of faith immortal meet,
And chastened sorrow, and remembrance sweet,
And greeting peace, and loyalty renewed,
And reverence, and praise, and gratitude,
And love, thro' winter's frost and summer's bloom
With tender gifts come pilgrims to his tomb.
There, 'neath the shadow of familiar walls,
With nearer voice his benediction falls,
While yet, with vaster view of things below,
He marks our warfare, hails each noble blow,
And calls from heights through holy struggles won
" Be strong, my children ! Let the work go on ! "

Reminiscence by Rev. H. H. Kelsey of the class of '79.

I have been asked to refer to the transitional period of the Seminary's history. I suppose this topic was given to me because it was my good fortune to be connected with the Seminary for two or three years on each side of its transition from Prospect to Broad Streets. It was my fortune, or my *fate*, to be present when the Seminary moved—a fortune, perhaps, since there was given me, a lot granted to but few mortals—to see a theological seminary " on wheels." It certainly was a *fate* to be so situated that your conscience compelled you to help *lift* the Seminary on wheels, especially when the major part of her material movable substance consisted of *books*. I helped moved the library twice; in 1877, when we moved 6,700 vols. from 33 to 46 Prospect St.; in 1880, when we moved 12,000 vols. to Broad St. We hope the time is not far distant when somebody will be obliged to move 40,000 vols. into a new and permanent home.

We left Prospect St., not with regrets, but with many pleasant, tender, sacred memories. We students had a good time there. We doubt if our successors in their present generous and beautiful home have a better. There was a peculiar social ease and freeness of life in those habitations of a departed aristocracy. I think, too, that there was a little flavor of social distinction in the atmosphere of the place which we felt. Prospect St. was once the court street of Hartford, and the most famous house on the street was the Wadsworth mansion in which we lived. It was the home of Col. Jeremiah Wadsworth, known in Revolutionary history as an efficient officer of the army, and a trusted friend of Washington. Whenever

Washington was in this region the Wadsworth house was his home. When Benedict Arnold was committing his act of treason at West Point, Washington with Count de Rochambeau were enjoying the hospitality of Col. Wadsworth's board, in the very room which was our chapel and Hebrew recitation-room. The Day house, No. 48 Prospect St., where we dined and supped, was the home of Hon. Thomas Day, for many years Secretary of the State. His name appeared on all Fast Day and Thanksgiving proclamations, which always closed with the following words: " Servile labor and vain recreation, on said day, are by law prohibited. By His Excellency's command, Thomas Day, Sec'y."

These famous houses, had they been of the 15th century, might have been haunted, and have been thus doubly famous. For I doubt if there were in this country a better place for restless spirits than the unused attics, by-ways, and labyrinths of the Wadsworth house. I do not think we should have been much surprised, if, when we occasionally discovered some unknown room or unused passage, we had found it inhabited. There was enough of the famous, the romantic, and ghostly about the place to make it interesting. I think we students had a better time there than the professors. No rooms could be much more unsuitable for lecture-rooms than were those guest-chambers of the Wadsworth mansion. They were small, the light was bad, and the ventilation—usually there wasn't any. But in spite of the infelicities we cherish the memory of Prospect Street. We cherish the memory of the earnest, devotional spirit and life of the students. Our life was free, hearty, and sometimes full of frolic. Our religious life, too, was hearty and natural. Evening prayer about the tables in the dining-room ! It was family prayer. We lived close to each other. Then there was the prayer-meeting on Saturday evening, when we retired from the supper-table into the room adjoining, and together confessed our sins to God,— and sometimes to each other: rehearsed our experiences, named our difficulties and needs, and cried to God for help: and always remembered in our prayers those of our number who had gone for the Sunday to preach, and all who had gone out from the Seminary to preach the Gospel. Such a spirit of devotion and healthy earnestness I have never felt elsewhere. This student prayer-meeting is one of the elements of this Seminary's present influence; one of the sources of its spiritual success.

Were there time I should like to speak of those dining-room scenes. When I was in the Seminary we had a number of "characters" among us, and not infrequently "things were lively." I would not have you infer that there is any want of character among the students at the present time. But perhaps "character," if odd or witty, was discovered more then than now in the dining-room. The council was usually "by itself," and individualism always found an expression. Once a year a dinner was given to the Faculty and resident Trustees. We then showed our dignity—and good appetites. Good appetites, however, were never wanting, for "Margaret" and "Kate" were a part of the corporation and governing body of the institution, and a good dinner was one of the certainties of each day's experience. Never a shadow of a fear of the dyspeptic fiend on Prospect St.!

When we moved we left behind us discomforts many, humiliations many, but pleasures many as well. In the Wadsworth house we had tugged lustily at tough Hebrew roots; we had learned the use of the Greek aorist. There we had been admonished and instructed by our professors in regard to family government. There we laughed, there we prayed, there we together sung hymns of praise. There we together bowed in sorrow, as we bore thence the form of one who loved this Seminary as she was herself loved by all who knew her. Sacred memories, these, of sacred seasons, never to be forgotten!

But when we moved we were more busied with our anticipations. The future was more to us then than the past. How faithfully we superintended the building of this Hall the carpenters will all bear witness. We were anxious to move. Delays were extremely tedious. We came to this new home with great expectations. In nothing were we disappointed. We were grateful to God for his goodness. We were grateful to our benefactor who gave us this beautiful home, whose venerable form we all reverently followed to its last resting-place. We, of the transitional period, rejoiced, and do rejoice greatly in the rapidly-increasing influence of this our beloved Seminary. We join you all in the congratulations of this happy anniversary, and we pray now as ever for the prosperity and peace of our Alma Mater.

EXTRACTS FROM LETTERS.

The following selection has been made from the many letters presented by Rev. W. S. Hawkes, of the Committee of Correspondence, who introduced the reading of extracts from them with this explanation:

"Many answers have been received to the circular which was sent to the alumni for reminiscences of their seminary life. The following extracts from these letters give a fair picture of successive periods in the Seminary's history as it now abides in memory. It is proposed to deposit all these letters in the alumni alcove of the library for future reference. Through the kindness of Rev. Dr. A. C. Thompson, we have also been permitted to quote from letters received by him from our foreign missionary alumni."

Rev. Professor Philip Schaff, D.D.

The following letter from Prof. Schaff pleasantly prefaces the reminiscences of the alumni, some of whom were his pupils when he was a lecturer in the Institute:

AMERICAN BIBLE REVISION COMMITTEE,
NEW YORK, May 2.

My Dear Dr. Thompson:

Nothing would give me greater pleasure than to participate in the semi-centenary festivities of Hartford Theological Seminary, which I had the honor and pleasure to serve as a lecturer on "Church History" for several years, and whose growing importance and prosperity I have followed with great satisfaction to this day. It is now one of the very best theological institutions of the country, and has a great future before it. I count it a great privilege that I was permitted to secure for it one professor and to recommend two others, who have proved efficient and faithful teachers of sound theology.

Unfortunately I am unable to attend, as I expect to sail for Europe May 7th, and am just now overwhelmed with examinations, preparations, and all sorts of work. But my heart will be with you, and my best wishes and prayers for yourself, your colleagues, and your institution, to which you have devoted your life.

I am, my dear Dr. Thompson,
Most truly yours,
PHILIP SCHAFF.

Congratulatory Note from the President of Middlebury College.

MIDDLEBURY, May 20, 1884.
My Dear Dr. Thompson:

Allow me to send you my Christian congratulations on the semi-centennial which you have celebrated.

The history of the Seminary is a noble and instructive one. God does not forsake his servants who persevere unto the end. The Seminary has had its dark days, but now the heavens are clear and bright. Your own connection with it is unique. Prof. Packard of Bowdoin College is the only case I know of that can compare with it. To work half a century for and in one institution has been given to very few. You may well say: "Bless the Lord, O my soul, and all that is within me bless His holy name."

Very sincerely yours,
C. HAMLIN.

Josiah Wolcott Tuner, '36, Strongville, O.

Among all the letters received scarcely one is written in a firmer, clearer hand than that of the only student on the ground at the laying of the corner-stone of the first Seminary building at East Windsor Hill, now in his 73d year. And it is cause for congratulation that we should have his full and interesting reminiscences:

"It was my privilege to be present at the ceremonies of laying the corner-stone of the first Seminary building; also to hear the inaugural address of Dr. Tyler. I shall never forget how the venerable Dr. Perkins of West Hartford was led through the crowd to the consecrated spot, and there, with trembling hands and voice, but with a firm faith, laid the foundation. . . . . Dr. Tyler was the only professor or teacher present, unless it were Dr. Nettleton, and I happened to be the only student then on the ground, and was probably the only spectator, from out of town, now living. Soon after this, however, other students came; first Brother Ellery Tyler and John Goddard; then Goodale, Perry, Payne, Haven, and Ives. For some time Dr. Tyler was our only instructor, but he was a host in himself, and one whose memory will ever be fondly cherished by his pupils. Not long after came our loved and now venerable Professor Thompson,—then young and vigorous. How he put us to digging up the tough Hebrew roots, himself leading the way! . . . . In due order came Dr. Coggswell, leading us through the realm of ecclesiastical history, ever swayed by the profoundest enthusiasm for his own department. In a good sense he always 'magnified his office.' If last, by no means least, came Dr. Nettleton. His 'familiar talks,' as he modestly persisted in calling them, were among the best and most practical lectures we were privileged to hear. . . . . They have been of great service to me all through my ministry, now of more than forty-seven years."

Lyman Whiting, '42, Cambridge, Mass.

" Sunset was just drawing its tinted web over the hushed elms, sandy roads, and the newish, lone, stately hall, the 'Seminary.' Four even brick stories — two front doors, orderly rows of cheerful windows, with a kindly, twilight smile on them. Inside are thirty students; and space plenteous for each. President Tyler, Professors Coggswell and Thompson, the teachers. An 'assistant' just home from Germanland, scholarlike, choice, and winning as a new Hebrew Chrestomathy,— was Augustus C. Thompson, A.M. He taught all manner of wisdom between Aleph and the Hithpāel. Some student voiced the ' morning prayer.' At evening the loved teachers, a patriarchal group, came in and led us.

"Dr. Tyler's lectures, made for his Portland pulpit, kept the grasp, throb, and almost *pulpit wrestling* in them as at first. In the chapel pulpit, his 'strength and beauty,' his flash and flame, were seen and felt. A master in Israel, truly, he was.

"Dr. Coggswell strode through church history somewhat as we fancy a Yantic Sachem roamed along the meadows of the big river beside which we dwelt. The 'old theology' got illumined in his free, fervid, gushing colloquies with us.

"The Melancthon of that era sat with us in Greek Testament Exegesis and Biblical Literature. But his garland is not yet all woven. Daily Dr. Nettleton came to sit awhile with the President. He was clean in person, so tidy in attire; each foot-fall a nicety; the face so apostolic, the eye ceaseless in recognitions, and a little like the fabled ancient ring, which took a copy of *the inside of each heart* its facets were turned upon. Wondrous man; more a vision then, than 'one like us.' So silent, almost speechless! Once I heard him *read*, inimitably, in the Scriptures."

Hiram Day, '42, *Glencoe, Cook Co., Ill.*

. . . . "When I was ready for my theological studies I wrote Dr. Tyler inquiring if the theology of Edwards and Dwight was taught in the Theological Institute of Connecticut. In reply Dr. Tyler inclosed to me the creed of the Institute; and it was all right. . . . . Dr. Tyler was to me the model instructor in theology. Dr. Coggswell was my teacher in church history; and he taught well, and only failed to convince any of my class that Adam could not talk until God had taught him to do so by talking to him. . . . . The course of instruction in the theological department of the Institute . . . . was plain, scriptural, and never unfair or belligerent in the treatment of contrary opinions. . . . . If this Seminary hereafter shall hold the same system of doctrinal faith, it shall be found for a long time to come that its mission is unchanged, its service not yet completed. . . . . I regard it as a great favor of Providence that I was directed to our beloved alma mater in theology."

Henry Beach Blake, '44.

"My memories of Dr. Nettleton, which are quite vivid, are of his sick bed. I was asked one vacation to spend a night with him, which I did. He seemed to take a fancy to me as a night watcher, and sent for me often. I spent many a night with him.

"'The chamber where the good man meets his fate
Is privileged beyond the common walk
Of virtuous life;—quite in the verge of heaven.'

"He slept little; talked a great deal. The scenes in which he was an actor in the great revivals through which he had passed were always very vivid, and the impressions were very vivid to me.

"His expositions of Scripture were many, incisive, original. One night we heard a cock crowing, and he said the selection of the crowing of a cock as the sign of the fall and penitence of Peter was an evidence of the Divine Wisdom of the Master. He said the common opinion that cocks crow only at certain times in the night, was erroneous. But the cock was a domestic bird among all nations, and that in all ages, to the end of time, and to the uttermost parts of the earth, lonely watchers in the silent hours would be reminded of the incident in Peter's history, and led to solemn thought upon unseen and eternal things.

"I have always deemed the impressions received from Dr. Nettleton, during the months and years he lay dying in that hallowed chamber, as among the most valued results of my theological course."

Thomas Henderson Rouse, '50, Paia, Maui, Hawaiian Islands.

"It was in the fall of '47 that I came to the old Seminary. I found it a large, lonely, four-story brick building, with a chapel beside it, on a quiet, elm-lined street, which was ankle deep with sand for miles, overlooking the valley of the Connecticut, with its thrifty farms and waving orchards.

"The place was still and lonely. At long intervals a carriage passed or a loaded cart filed in from the meadows. The arrival of the evening stage, on its way to Broad Brook, was the stirring event of the day. Then the students turned out and the professors took their evening stroll. It was our only connection with the busy world without. It brought our papers, our new books, which were distributed from Mr. Charlton's store, with many a graceful bow, and liquid, meandering remarks of compliment or sympathy, from the gracious old gentleman. The lightning trains sped by in the far distance over the Connecticut, reached only by a lazy, rope ferry, tooted up by a tin horn.

"It was a good place to study. You *had* to study. There was absolutely nothing else to do. Not a sight or sound to excite or distract the mind, except the songs of the robins and meadow larks. If you did not study you would die with ennui. The carpenter's shop, where we planned out bookcases, and the garden weedy, and full of everlasting quackgrass, soon cloyed on our enterprise. I needed no outward pressure to drive me to study afterwards. The habits of quiet investigation formed there have stuck by me.

"At 11 o'clock the bell sounded for lectures, the door of the President's mansion opened, and he moved slowly down the walk, crossed the street, and, with his manuscript under his arm, ascended to the lecture-room. He seemed at first look the embodiment of a sound and well-rounded theology. A dozen or fifteen students, often less, filed in about the same time. When all were seated, a short invocation was addressed to 'The greatest and best of Beings'—the doctor's peculiar phrase, and the lecture commenced. The old doctor sat in delivery. His tones at first were deep, low, and deliberate, varied with a peculiar emphasis, when he closed some ponderous sentence, as a clencher to his argument. As he proceeded he waxed more earnest, as the visions of Taylorism and the New-Light heresies, with their destructive innovations, rose to view between the lines of his manuscript, and the pent energies fired his delivery. His face flushed, the big veins in his lofty forehead swelled to whipcords, his right arm became impatient, and his clenched hand ploughed slowly but intensely along the table, and every word seemed to weigh a solid pound, as he drove into us the good, old, biblical theology. He generally remained sitting awhile like a patriarch, inviting the confidence of his pupils, who crowded around with question or request.

"In Greek and Hebrew we had Dr. Thompson. In recitation he was tender of your crude expositions,—scarcely ever directly disputing you,—and in his correction saved all he consistently could of your rendering. But the veteran professor and venerable dean is still among us,—the last of the Seminary fathers,—and I forbear. I speak of him as he was thirty-six years ago, hair black and bushy, covering a grand forehead and deep-set eyes. But now the granite gray crowns that self-poised brain, solid and well in hand, while beneath is a heart true to you and true to duty. '*In coelum serus redeat.*'

"The sweet, amiable, gentle Dr. Hooker was also a member of the faculty while I was there. In his pulpit prayers he was most tender and touching. Poor man, he knew too well how to enter into some of life's deepest trials, for he had that greatest of sorrows, a wife insane. In his addresses at a throne of grace there always came, in tones of touching tenderness, the petition for those 'That had diseases of the mind.' From this source there came sorrow upon sorrow. There was living with him at East Windsor a daughter; tall, beautiful, accomplished,—a very angel with infolded wings, of a spirit so devoted and tender, heavenly and sad withal, that her walk among us was like some superior being, the shadow of whose coming and going filled us with a kind of awe. She had spoken of herself as a shadow on her home, and other expressions of deep despondency, when like a shock and a deep shadow indeed, the news came on a dark winter morning, bitter cold, that she was missing. The searchers traced her footsteps to the frozen river. From under the ice they drew her lifeless form, carried it to the home she had graced, and from thence to its last resting-place. Well might that father say, ' There are no sorrows like unto my sorrows.' We all felt so, in our weak faith. But he, so nearly sanctified, only drew nearer to the side of God, like a child fully weaned, saying, ' My Father, Thy will be done.'

" Next to the professors about the old Seminary, we oftenest saw that careful, shrewd, conscientious old Yankee farmer, Deacon Ellsworth, lay defender of the faith. There was always a sly, watchful, half suspicious, yet genial smile on his honest face, as he came looking about the halls and buildings, as though he loved his boys dearly, yet thought they would bear watching,—were not wholly lifted above the liability to sins,—of carelessness, at least; and I think that was the case. He frowned a little when he found the doors slamming in the wind, the blinds shattering themselves against the brick walls, the gates going to pieces, and the tools lost from the work-shop, and other indications of a general heedlessness. Precious old Seminary sentinel! His carefulness taught us care and economy, and how to combine shrewdness with thrift, and, when he died, a pang came over us that we had not been more careful of the sacred pence committed to his keeping. ' A faithful man who can find.' Oh! Psalmist, if you had lived in these latter days, and had known Deacon Ellsworth, you need not have despaired."

Robert Dexter Miller, '52, West Hartford, Vt.

" Dr. Bennett Tyler always appears in the foreground of my recollections. . . . .

" At the close of our graduating exercises . . . . he happened to meet a number of students, gathered in front of the Seminary buildings, and was somehow led into giving us a short sketch of his life. He said, after nineteen years of earnest devotion to the interests of this new enterprise, that he had never had a doubt of its having been the way of duty for him to leave the large, united, prosperous church in Portland, and take and hold the place he has since occupied;—a place of comparative difficulty, discouragement, and apparent uncertainty. I well recall how happy the great, good man seemed to be.

"Prof. Gale, our Professor in Ecclesiastical History, who of us has ever felt like saying anything but good of him, so genial, companionable, and helpful? Those many practical suggestions of his on subjects pertaining to the gospel minister's office-work, given so pleasantly in off-hand lecture-room talks; who that enjoyed them has forgotten them, or failed of making them largely profitable as a pastor in doing wisely and effectively the duties of that high calling?"

William Brown Lee, '53.

"I remember that one day in the early fall of 1850, I took an old rattle-to-bang stage at the American hotel in Hartford, and went to East Windsor. I was landed on the sidewalk with my trunks, in front of the old Seminary buildings, and came very near to getting into a muddle with the stage-driver, because he would not take my trunks to my room. That driver was a citizen of East Windsor, and knew, and carefully maintained, and defended his accustomed rights. While I was musing on the steps a huge form came rolling across the street from the president's house, and soon the genial Dr. Tyler grasped me by the hand and gave me a warm welcome. The Rev. Dr. Thompson soon called on me, and in his gentle manner and kind spirit, made me begin to feel very much at home. I called Dr. Tyler, Paul; and Dr. Thompson, John; appellations which my fellow-students will remember cleaved to our beloved professors.

"I had purposed to stay in East Windsor only a single year, and then go to Princeton; but got so in love with Tyler, and Thompson, and Gale, and Lawrence, and Hooker, that I abandoned the plan of going away. We cast the world behind our backs, and let it wag in its own way, while we gave ourselves to study and to prayer; to discussions, to lectures and debates; to cutting and splitting our own wood; to gardening in the large and beautiful garden back of the Seminary; and to mechanical pursuits in the carpenter house; but I never knew anyone to overwork either in garden or carpenter shop. We used to go on long rambles, and often on rides to Hartford. We played daily, in good weather, at the game of loggerheads, by which we nearly ruined the lawn, much to the discomforture of good Deacon Ellsworth; peace to his ashes. Ours was a thorough country life."

Benjamin Parsons, '54, Windham, Greene County, N. Y.

. . . . "The three years I spent in study at the Theological Institute at East Windsor Hill were agreeable to me. . . . . My ambition, spurred on by the proffer of a pecuniary prize to the candidate passing the best examination in theology as taught (in Latin) by Francois Turretin, led me to supplement, for two years, my study of English works on theology, with diligent study of the methodical and terse writings of that distinguished successor of John Calvin. The gaining of the whole prize for the first, and half of it for the second year, was, of trivial importance, compared with the broadening and deepening and solidifying of views which resulted from that study, and for which I can never be too grateful.

"Our life at the Hill was, of course, not eventful. . . . . In the meantime, however, we were not so isolated but that the woes and wants of a world 'dead in trespasses and sins,' could and did reach us, making a mighty appeal. . . . . So strong was the interest at one time, that several members of the class of 1853 seemed very likely to devote themselves to labor in foreign lands. I think, however, that only Rev. Charles Hartwell went abroad. In my own class, that of 1854, the missionary spirit prevailed to such an extent that Carlton went to Siam, Adams to Africa, (dying soon after his arrival, and dying in the triumphs of faith,) Maccussohn to the Jews of Greece, and myself to the Armenians of Asia Minor. My missionary life covered a period of only six years, and those were six of the brightest and happiest of my life. Among the items which contributed to make them such, I found the pleasure of *knowing* that I *was* doing good, added to the pleasure of endeavoring to do good. Here is, I think, an advantage which the foreign missionary has over many a hard-working and equally faithful laborer in our land. . . . .

"I see no good reason why, from an institution so manned there should *ever* be graduated a single specimen of the order of kid-gloved sentimentalist, place-seeking adventurer, presumptuous, or barely half-fledged theologian."

Moses Thurston Runnels, '56, *Sanbornton, N. H.*

"A former pastor of mine in southern New Hampshire, being a New Haven graduate, exclaimed to a friend, on hearing that I was about to become a student at East Windsor: 'Don't let him go there! don't let him go there!! They are behind the age;—and behind every age.'

"I have never heard of a course in theology in any institution which I would have willingly exchanged for that of Dr. Tyler's. Once in a week our three professors were accustomed to meet all the students of an evening and talk to us in a familiar way of special topics which might prove of practical advantage to us in the ministry, drawing largely from their own experience. The hints thrown out at those gatherings have been of incalculable benefit to me all through my course, thus far.

"Dea. Erastus Ellsworth was our honored lay-father. His interest in us was unbounded and genuine. He looked after our physical wants and comforts. He kept the ample wood-shed well stocked with good wood which he sold us at the lowest cost price, encouraged us to work it up ourselves for exercise, and furnished our rooms with Franklin stoves, by whose open fires we took a world of comfort and enjoyment. He was also glad to have us choose our plats in the garden back of the Seminary buildings in the summer, affording us every facility for bodily exercise in that line. My own carrot bed used to yield me $15 each season, besides a margin for flowers. Directly back of the Seminary grounds was pasture, with a pleasant footpath extending to the Connecticut.

Here was my favorite walk, and on the river's bank I had a secluded spot for 'vocal gymnastics.' At the commencement of my third year there was a general stampede of students from East Windsor to other institutions, especially Andover. Their excuse was that if they remained they should be graduating from a 'Decaying Institution,' and this would prove an incubus on their future prospects. I, for one, could not so grieve the heart of that sainted man, Rev. Bennett Tyler, D.D., who combined with his massiveness of intellect and theological erudition, the simplicity of a little child."

Henry M. Bridgman, '60, Umgumbi Station, Southeast Africa.

"My poor, short-lived memory will, I fear, be of little use to the well-filled Hartford Seminary of to-day, palpitating with a life rooted in the eternal, the essential truths of Revelation,—a life not less scholarly than spiritual.

"My short residence at East Windsor Hill was in the last days of the beloved Tyler. I can never forget the drizzly day we went out and sang a hymn as we laid him in his tomb. My days at East Windsor Hill were pleasant days. The students were equal to the twelve disciples *in number*. At least three of them not only longed to meet the heathen but did meet them—Robbins, Pease, and Bridgman. Another student was so fully in accord with these brothers that it was thought best to send him for a time into the 'hill country,' Westhampton. Then (that he might be fully equipped as a good soldier) into the 'low country' about Port Hudson. And he took not only his church but his prayer-meeting with him. Then, to further perfect him for his future work, we allowed him to labor among the hoodlums of San Francisco. After a few years we felt sure he would answer to send forward to Honolulu,—the outskirts of the heathen world. As he still felt himself unfitted for the heathen (Simon Pure) we sent him to Germany, thinking that a sojourn in the land of lager beer and sound scholarship, with the writing of an excellent book on 'The History of the Bible,' would thoroughly prepare him either to go to the heathen in person or incite others, provided he could only take *one more course of study* at Hartford Seminary. *There* you will now find this brother, doing most excellent work, as Rev. Prof. Bissell.

"Here is my confession. I spent the last two years of my theological course at Union Seminary, New York. As things *were* I do not regret it; but as things *are* at Hartford, could I live life over again, and I could pass the examination for entrance (which is doubtful) I would enter at Hartford. As it is not given to men to live their lives over again, except in vain regrets, I will tell you what I plan to do. 'In place of the fathers are their children.' I have one at Amherst, and propose to send him to Hartford Seminary, provided you head him, at the end of his theological course, to 'the dark continent.'"

John Otis Barrows, '63.

I got my beginning at East Windsor. It was a right beginning. If any of us failed to make the progress we should have made it was because South Windsor was too near 'the Hill.' The only regret I have is that occasionally I gave way to youthful weakness and took moonlight walks to South Windsor, while Kal and Niphal, Hiphil, and Hophal were waiting to rise up in judgment against me the next morning. So long as it was dark, or even under the light of a lamp, the full form, the indefinable hideousness of these grim old warriors of Jewish origin failed to make a due impression upon my blunted sensibilities; but with the morning light there was no strength in me. An encounter was out of the question. Only the kind consideration of my indulgent teacher kept me alive. If we gave less attention than we ought to theology, it was because of the distracting influences of the political condition of the country. Civil war with all its terrors came upon us. There was a student among us all of whose friends and nearest relatives were in the Confederate service. Yet Charles C. Painter stood firm. His hands first caught the rope when a flag was raised on the Seminary building.

Edward Trumbell Hooker, '63, *Charleston, South Carolina.*
Dear Brothers Hallock and Hawkes:
"A wanton fancy asks if the names of all the alumni have H and K in them like yours and mine. Just there I remember my father meeting at anniversary time two members of the Pastoral Union, whose names were the same, and greeting them with an extended hand to each as "two Hydes," received the unexpected, quick rejoinder with a laugh, "Yes, and the horns are generally not far off!" That was the pattest pun upon his name that Father Hooker ever suffered. But there were other letters of the alphabet in those days. Two graduates once came at anniversary time to our door and introduced each other to the stranger who happened to open it, as Mr. Knight and Mr. Day.

"I could begin with the journey in 1844 of the new 'Professor of Homiletics and Ecclesiastical History,' with his family, from Bennington, Vt., via Springfield, Mass., whence we took, before the days of the railroad, a little stern-wheel steamboat, through the wonderful Windsor Locks, to the old Bissell Ferry landing under the pines at the edge of the beautiful meadows, back of our future home. There was music and social liveliness with sometimes serious intent, when the sisters and the students together passed the summer evenings, or boated on the smooth Connecticut, or rode to Wadsworth Tower.

"Then I see, as if really there again, that ornamentally partitioned garden in the rear of the Seminary, whose chief products were melons for the tempted gamins of the town; the cruciform arbor above the frog-pool and terraces; the open belfry on the roof of the Seminary, frequent resort of lovers of that charming landscape. I could itemize the (wide) pits, where *loggerheads* were literally played, as I have never seen elsewhere; the veritable chopping-block, where, some one having given him a long swallow-tailed coat, Bro. Goodwin's classmates abridged said tails with an ax, having seated him in position, *vi et armis*. That was Goodwin the violinist; and that is a true story.

"There was Lee of fascinating social vein; and Bacon full of fun; Knight, who criticised a labored sermon of Bacon's, read with firm confidence in its greatness, with the sententious 'Humph, pious words!'

"You mention first, of course, among historic names, Tyler. He was to me the Seminary. A lad still, I remember his wrapt prayers, which had no need to keep always shut the trembling eyelids, that showed the uplifted eyes as in the picture of John Huss. With what white-souled vehemence he preached vital truth behind that desk in the little chapel, there are many that can testify. He was to me a Boanerges; but a gentle one, with his small white fist (for so large a man) emphasizing his clear sentences upon the open Bible.

"Josiah Tyler, now long in Africa, of whom there, his father said, he had more joy than at home, reached the climax of description of a certain man's soundness, when he said he was orthodox, *tremendous orthodox; more orthodox than father!*' 'Language could no farther go.' The corner-stone of the Theological Institute of Connecticut, which was the doorstone of Jonathan Edward's father's home, in the lower town, was the rock in the sea, on which the cross seemed to stand unmoved.

"I must not, could not, forget Dea. Ellsworth, the modest but tenacious 'Professor of Brick and Mortar,' as he styled himself, who placed that stone, and saw that everything was built afterwards to the delight of a thorough mechanic's heart, who rejoiced in his work as done 'upon honor' as '*pro Christo et ecclesiae.*'"

Albert Warren Clark, '68, *Prague, Austria.*

"I rejoice in the prosperity of Hartford Seminary because I believe she is doing honest, manly work on abiding foundations. In these times we need the clear, unwavering tone of an institution not troubled about theological *may-bes*, a school of the prophets not ashamed of the time-worn, battle-worn banner of a crucified and risen Christ."

Winfield Scott Hawkes, '68, *South Hadley Falls, Mass.*

" I was the first new student on the ground at Hartford. Harmon of '67 was the only other man in the building that night Oct. 5, 1865. The next morning early I heard a voice ringing through the passages and vacant rooms of that spacious old Wadsworth mansion, singing

"' I'm monarch of all I survey.'

"Whatever I am as a minister of the Lord Jesus, I owe to Dr. Vermilye, more than to any one man. It but faintly expresses my feeling to say that I revere and honor his memory. If any student left his teaching without being able to state his own views definitely, whether in accord with Dr. Vermilye's or not, it was solely his own fault. Dr. Vermilye had no superiors in the art of putting things clearly and logically. I noticed several classes pass through the experience of earnestly antagonizing his teaching in the junior year, but came through the middle year accepting it, and the senior year warm and loyal admirers of the man and his system of theology. In the work of the ministry I have found no occasion to change my faith. What I was taught at Hartford stands the test of real life and work."

Isaac Curtis Meserve, '69, *New Haven, Conn.*

" Dr. Vermilye's class-room was the place where everything was done with pains-taking fidelity and in reverent love of truth. Discussions sometimes made the sparks fly; but they only served to make a halo for this kind-hearted teacher. Dr. Vermilye did not ask his classes to accept his theology without examination, nor did he pretend that his—or any—system of Christian doctrine was, or could be, absolutely complete and inflexible. He stimulated our minds to enthusiastic work; but he insisted continually, and uncompromisingly, that God's Word is the final test and arbiter of all belief. It is probable that all his students became as fixed as himself in that axiom."

Martin Kellogg Pasco, Brownton, Minn.

"I understand there is a good, new, first-class gymnasium now. Little did I think that such a thing would grow out of the little seed which I planted. You remember the old barn back of the Day house. I conceived the idea of tearing out the inside and putting in those few pieces of apparatus. I can quote without blushing the well-known sentence, ' *Quorum pars magna fui.*' Bliss, and Meserve, and Miles, and Morris, and others helped and did as much as I did; but I shall modestly claim the credit of the germ. I cherish the memory of the year I spent at Hartford."

Edward Sackett Hume, '75, Bombay, India.

"The three years spent at Hartford Theological Seminary were altogether the pleasantest and most profitable of my whole educational course.

"It would be impossible for instructors to take a deeper interest in the students under their care than was taken by our professors in me and my fellow-students; not only so, but we were encouraged to live on such terms of *intimacy* with them that we could esteem them our warmest friends. I regard this as one of the important features of the Hartford Seminary. I sincerely hope the time may never come when the professors of this institution will cease to be intimate with the students. I cannot refrain from speaking of the weekly conferences which gave each professor an opportunity of discoursing to us in a familiar way on various subjects. Some of these were very profitable. One of the professors used to speak often on the importance of private devotions, and in that connection used an expression which passed among us students as a proverb, ' The morning hour, gentlemen, the morning hour.' The gesture used when speaking these words is, I doubt not, remembered by many. This advice came with peculiar fitness from one whom we saw pass the building in which we lived at an early hour in all kinds of weather, on his way to his study, where many an hour, as we all knew, was spent in prayer."

George Samuel Pelton, '77, *Omaha, Neb.*

"The Theological Institute of Connecticut is a part of my life. Born within rifle's shot of the old buildings at East Windsor Hill, I grew alongside of it. To me, a poor farmer's boy, it was a constant inspiration. The daily passing of the students, the Sunday services, the preaching by the professors, the Sabbath-school—all these were wrought into my daily life; and many a time I vowed in my boyish zeal that, God helping me, I would become a member of the institution and enjoy all the delightful benefits that my imagination pictured the happy denizens of the school as enjoying.

"How well I remember Dr. Tyler's portly form and kindly face; and Dr. Lawrence, the genial Scotchman, who always prayed 'that the Word of God might be like apples of gold in pictures of silver' to those who listened. How well I remember the day upon which its removal to Hartford was determined; the sadness that fell on the community; the grief of one of its firmest and truest friends, Dea. Ellsworth, who gave of his time, and substance, and prayers most bountifully. Of its incalculable worth to me when a student in the institution at Hartford I can never say enough. It was here under wise men that my theology was straightened out for all time. Dr. Thompson, Dr. Childs, Dr. Riddle, and Dr. Karr—to all these I owe a debt of everlasting gratitude."

Charles Sylvester Sanders, '79, *Aintab, Turkey.*

"I knew the Seminary only by name before I went there; did not even know that it was an old-school Seminary. I have never been anything but thankful that I went. I was there in the 'ford of passage' period and the passing years do not (in my own mind and feelings) carry the Seminary across the city. The course of instruction is in my recollections a source of unmixed satisfaction. I am more and more convinced that our Seminary does wisely in extending exegesis and history through the course instead of concentrating the study of them, the one in the earlier and the other in the latter part of the curriculum.

"The religious atmosphere of the Seminary is a thing I remember with much pleasure. Last of all, I have no need of changing my theological opinions; and am as ready now as ever to subscribe with no 'mental reservations' to the creed of the Seminary. I am glad that signing with 'mental reservation' went by its proper name—dishonesty—in our Seminary.

"I accept the new theology heartily, as far as it consists (as defined by its organs) in making Christ all in all as supreme in our theology; but it annoys me to hear this spoken of as a new discovery, for it was the spirit of all the theological instruction, or other instruction, that I ever received in that dreadful old-school Seminary, the Theological Institute of Connecticut."

From a letter to Dr. A. C. Thompson we are permitted to quote the following:

"I arrived at the Seminary six weeks after the opening of the course. That very night there was a conference at which Prof. Riddle remarked, or rather gave us to understand, that 'broad culture does not mean spread out thin;' also some very pointed suggestions *not to preach* until we were licensed. The more experience I have the more I admire the attitude of our professors on that point. 'Don't grind until you get something into your hopper,' even now remains fast in memory. Very soon we learned that 'if a man stuck to his aorists, he would be proof against more than half the heresies in existence.' We have tried to stick faithfully, not only to aorists, but also to all parts of Greek grammar. We were very fortunate in having an opportunity to study Mr. Moody and his methods for a month. I should say also very fortunate in being where we could hear so great a variety of preaching as in Hartford. I do not sympathize with any institution, or individual, that goes around with a chip on its, or his shoulder, and spoiling for a fight. Hartford Seminary is singularly free from this,—at least, Hartford Seminary, as I know it. While private opinions were freely expressed, the attitude of the Seminary strikes me as altogether a proper attitude for a seminary to take. While we were there, there was the utmost freedom in investigation, but no mercy toward any one who held advanced opinions, merely for the sake of differing, without being well persuaded in his own mind. As I understand the spirit of the Seminary it was well expressed in a remark of Dr. Riddle's one morning in our Greek class: ' I don't care whether you agree with me or not, but if you don't I'm going to be sure that you have a reason for disagreeing with me, and that you know *why* you disagree with me.'"

William W. Sleeper, '81.

" The training now given in Hartford is so truly evangelistic,—so thoroughly grounded in God's Word, and yet so broad in details,—that none of the recent alumni, at least, can venture to blame his Seminary, if he find himself engaged in other than missionary work. It is my earnest conviction that Hartford's new departure in the line of furnishing a practical musical education is an important and praiseworthy one. For the missionary, the drill received there is of immense advantage; and it cannot be much less for any minister. Perhaps the best idea I received from the Seminary is, that faithful study of the Inspired Records in their original tongues can best furnish the Christian minister with the weapons he will need in his warfare against sin."

Paul Ansel Chadbourne, '51.

This touching evidence of the dying remembrance of Dr. Chadbourne has been reserved as the most fitting conclusion of these reminiscences:

" Dr. Chadbourne's brief connection with this Seminary was long enough to awaken a deep desire for its highest prosperity, and lasting affection for its officers—Dr. Tyler, Dr. Gale, and your own Dr. Thompson—whom he valued among his most esteemed friends.

" His thoughts turned to you during the last week of his life, when in those days of physical suffering and exhaustion he knew that God had come to take him to Himself, and he remembered the institutions of learning in which he had studied and taught.

"To the students of this institution he sent a most urgent appeal, begging them to preach the Gospel of Christ in its purity, its simplicity, and its fullness. 'Tell them,' he said, 'that it would be better for each one to return to his home, and the doors of the Seminary to be closed forever, than for them to accept and teach anything but the truth as revealed in God's Word.'

"The exact words of that remarkable message it is impossible to repeat. It was feared by those who heard these utterances that they were the last that could fall from his lips; but in the early hours of the morning, following a night of alarming prostration, the words, 'Oh, the pain and agony of Calvary, and all for one,' were twice repeated by him; the tones of his voice indicating how fully he realized what the words signified; and then, in sweetest voice of earnest persuasion, he added, 'but this sacrifice was for all—for every one—whosoever will may come, He will turn none empty away.'

"He spoke of himself but once, when he said, 'Can it be possible that I am soon to sing the song of Moses and the Lamb!' and lifting up his hands he prayed: 'Oh, my God, give me strength to show forth Thy glory.'"

APPENDIX.

THE PASTORAL UNION.

The annual meeting of the Pastoral Union of Connecticut was held at Hosmer Hall on Thursday, May 8th, at 2 P. M. The Union, which founded and controls the Seminary, is composed of ministers of Connecticut and of other States, who are elected to membership one year after their nomination, and includes the ministers and laymen, who are annually chosen by the body to constitute its Board of Trustees, to whose trust the care and government of the institution are committed. By these means the Seminary is held in close and vital relation with the churches, to whose faith and will its Trustees and Faculty must ever be subservient.

The doctrinal basis of the organization coincides with the creeds long accepted by the Congregational churches of New England, which have ever been believed by the members of this Union to harmonize with the teachings of the Divine Word ascertained through study. Signature to these "Articles of Agreement" is a condition of membership in the Pastoral Union, and public assent to them is annually required by every member of the Faculty and Board of Trustees. Satisfactory testimonials of good standing in the membership of some Christian church of one of the evangelical denominations, are among the conditions demanded of each candidate for admission to the Seminary course. To defend revealed truth against wrong interpretations of Holy Writ and rationalistic theology, and to train candidates for the sacred office to be eminently Biblical preachers in loving devotion to the Master, was and is the governing purpose of the Pastoral Union in the founding and maintenance of the Seminary.

In addition to the routine business of the year the following matters of special interest are worthy of record:

An unusually large accession was made to the membership from the ministry of other States, and numerous nominations were reported for next year's election.

A committee was appointed to report at the next meeting a revision of the constitution and laws.

An amendment to the constitution was put upon its passage providing for the change of the name of the Seminary from "The Theological Institute of Connecticut" to "The Hartford Theological Seminary."

The following resolution was unanimously passed:

WHEREAS, For several years many citizens of Hartford have freely opened their homes and their houses to entertain such returning alumni, and this year their kindness has been taxed to an unusual degree; therefore,

Resolved, That we do hereby express our obligations to the many families of this city who have exercised an enlarged hospitality in entertaining the great number of alumni and other friends who have been present at this jubilee meeting. That so large a number of beautiful and hospitable homes have been so freely placed at our disposal, merits and receives our special gratitude. We venture to hope that those who have entertained are not without some recompense in enlarged knowledge of our affairs, our prosperity, our history, and our hope, and a still deeper interest in our institution, whose chief aim is the enrichment of the Christian ministry in our own and other lands, but which also aims to bless the city of its habitation and its love.

Resolved, That these resolutions be entered upon our records and be read at the public meeting this evening.

Rev. A. W. Hazen presented the annual statement of the Board of Trustees, which included the reports of the Faculty and instructors, the librarians and the examining committee given below, and also the following announcements:

Rev. E. B. Webb, D.D., of Boston, succeeded to the Presidency of the Board of Trustees made vacant by the resignation of Rev. Jeremiah Taylor, D.D.

The following resolution was unanimously passed by the board:

WHEREAS, The Rev. J. Taylor, D.D., after thirteen years of faithful service, has this day resigned his office as President of the Board of Trustees:

Resolved, We hereby record our cordial appreciation of the dignity and untiring fidelity with which he has presided over the meetings of the board, and served the Seminary in its varying emergencies.

Rev. Prof. Hartranft having resigned the office of Librarian, a warm vote of thanks was passed for the arduous and efficient services he has rendered the institution in this position. Rev. Ernest C. Richardson was elected his successor, and the office of Assistant Librarian, which he has so acceptably filled, was abolished.

Waldo S. Pratt, A.M., Instructor in Music and Voice Building, was elected Associate Professor of Ecclesiastical Music and Hymnology.

The proposal of Eldridge Torrey, in which Mrs. Miriam M. Thompson, Miss Martha C. Burgess, John N. Denison, and Hon. William Hyde joined, to donate five thousand dollars for the pecuniary foundation of a Lectureship on Foreign Missions, was thankfully accepted, and the professorship into which the donors hoped the lectureship would grow, is to be designated when established " The Professorship of Evangelistic Theology."

The purchase of the valuable building site situated on Broad street, between the Seminary property and Farmington avenue, was announced.

Efforts have been inaugurated for the establishment of a museum, together with a collection of such books, charts, maps, etc., as will afford the students an opportunity to become acquainted with the researches of archæologists, and investigations in the various departments of science. This is felt to be an important adjunct to their course of study, in order that they may be able to utilize the results of such investigations, in applying and defending the truth. For the furtherance of this project there have been found those who are willing to help with a liberal hand.

REPORT OF THE FACULTY

FOR THE YEAR ENDING MAY 8, 1884.

To the Board of Trustees of the Theological Institute of Connecticut:

BRETHREN: The year now closing with us, while marked by no events of extraordinary importance, has borne witness throughout to the continued favor of Almighty God. It can still be said, as it was said one year ago, that "the number of students has been larger than ever before in the history of the Seminary."

When the present Senior class entered, the whole number of students in the Seminary was twenty-eight. It is now forty-eight; or, including the advanced class, fifty-four. This remarkable growth, to whatever causes it may be ascribed, shows no signs as yet of being other than healthy and permanent. It remains to be seen what suitable response the friends of the institution will make to the heavier tasks and greater responsibilities which Divine Providence has thus laid upon it.

The advanced class, made up, with a single exception, of our own graduates, have pursued with fidelity, and for the most part, with gratifying progress, their studies according to the prescribed scheme. The presence among us of these young men of more mature powers, of settled religious convictions, and thoroughly loyal to the higher aims of the institution, has no doubt been of service in developing still further that harmony of feeling and marked *esprit de corps* which of late years have especially characterized the Hartford Seminary. The ordinary routine of recitations and other exercises of the undergraduate classes has been less interrupted during the present year than is often the case; while the regularity and punctuality of attendance, on the part of the great majority of students, have been worthy of special commendation. It is believed that the results of much faithful and conscientious work will not fail to appear in the written and oral examinations which conclude the studies of the year.

The health of the students, generally, during the term has been excellent. No case of prolonged illness has occurred where such illness was contracted here. This is due, under God, largely to regular habits, the favorable location and construction of the seminary building, wholesome food, and, especially, to the uniform practice of systematic physical exercise in the gymnasium, under the direction of a competent instructor. Attention is renewedly called, in this connection, to the accompanying report of Mr. E. A. Chase, who, as last year, has most satisfactorily conducted the exercises in this department. His table of comparative statistics, showing results in special cases, will awaken particular interest.

While referring you to the report of the Librarian for a more complete statement of the condition and needs of the library, it may be said here that the increase of books during the last twelve months, including some hundreds gained by exchange, has been upwards of four thousand, making the present total number somewhat over thirty-eight thousand. The most notable acquisition has been the "Beck collection" of works relating to Luther, which is doubtless unsurpassed in this country. The most obvious and pressing needs of the library at present are, first, a considerable enlargement in the direction of modern books; and, second, more ample quarters where these rich stores of information, now scattered here and there in various rooms, may become more readily accessible and be more conveniently used. The work of cataloguing, classifying, etc., has, with the help of students, gone steadily forward. There has also been a noticeable and gratifying increase in the use made of the library by members of the Seminary. Until the present year the small fund devoted to the purchase of books especially required by professors in their several departments, and to be retained in their rooms as long as needed, amounting to something less than two hundred dollars yearly, has not been drawn upon. It supplies a need which had come to be deeply felt.

At a meeting of the Faculty, held April 25th, the following resolutions were unanimously passed:

Resolved, That we recommend to the Trustees the appointment of Mr. Ernest C. Richardson as Librarian.

Resolved, That the office of Assistant Librarian be abolished.

Resolved, That the Librarian be required to subscribe to the creed of the Seminary, and to make the usual annual affirmation.

Resolved, That we recommend that the following addition be made to the article in the "Laws of the Institute," headed "Library," page 29, after the words "Prudential Committee": The Faculty shall annually appoint one of their number to act as an advisory committee, who shall be the final authority in all matters pertaining to the selection, exchange, purchase, and classification of books and periodicals. This committee shall also present an annual report to the Faculty, to be incorporated in the annual report of the Faculty to the Board of Trustees. The Librarian shall present his annual report directly to the Board of Trustees.

The report of Mr. Waldo S. Pratt, instructor in Music and Voice-Building, is herewith submitted. It will be seen how deservedly prominent a feature of our curriculum this department has become. The statistical summary of the number of hours given to individual training in voice-building, general exercises in singing, the regular and special rehearsals of the Choral Union, including three public performances, lectures to the several classes on the elements of music and hymnody, besides those given outside the Seminary, makes a record of unusual diligence, and it may be added, of marked faithfulness and success. Your attention is especially called to that feature of the report which sets forth the difficulty of properly combining elocutionary work with the musical. The Faculty are in full accord with the sentiment there expressed, and earnestly recommend the employment, as soon as practicable, of a competent teacher of elocution who shall give a sufficient portion of his time to the thorough instruction of our students in this branch.

We beg leave, also, to lay before you a resolution passed by the Faculty at a meeting held April 7th, to the effect that it being desirable, in our judgment, that Mr. Pratt's position in this institution be more distinctly defined and rendered more permanent, we respectfully recommend his appointment as Associate Professor of Ecclesiastical Music and Hymnology.

This Seminary, which has the honor of being represented by one of our colleagues on the committee of twenty-five designated by the National Council held in St. Louis in 1880 to prepare a creed and catechism for the denomination, has had at least the equal honor of dissenting from the final conclusions reached by the majority of the committee, the action of Dr. Karr in this respect having been approved by a unanimous vote of the Faculty.

We are about to celebrate the fiftieth anniversary of the existence and work of this institution. It is an occasion peculiarly fitted to awaken reflection and stimulate hope. If there were good and sufficient reasons for the founding of this Seminary in the midst of the New England churches of fifty years ago, there is certainly no less reason for continuing it and giving it the heartiest coöperation in the New England of to-day. Indeed, it seems to many that, whatever good it may have accomplished in the past, it has plainly, in the providence of God, come to its present prominence among institutions of this kind "for such a time as this." In the midst of wide-spread defection it abates nothing of its loyalty to the accredited historical standards of the denomination, or of its fidelity in teaching the undiminished, unadulterated Word of God.

May it not be confidently anticipated that those called upon to support the institution will see that in the generosity of its endowment, and the facilities it shall thus be enabled to offer for the best and most rewarding service, it does not fall short of the Providential demands now made upon it?

In behalf of the Faculty,
EDWIN C. BISSELL.
HARTFORD, May 1, 1884.

REPORT OF THE INSTRUCTOR IN MUSIC AND VOICE-BUILDING.

Mr. Waldo S. Pratt, the Instructor in Music and Voice-Building, presented a statistical summary of his work, from which we take simply the several headings under which the matter was grouped. These headings are, (1) Individual Training of the Juniors in Voice-Building, including the elements of both Singing and Speaking, with Exercises; (2) General Exercises for all the Students together in Singing Tunes, Chants, and Anthems, including Constant Practice in Sight-Reading; (3) Lectures to an Optional Class of Juniors upon the Rudiments of Music; (4) Lectures to all the Classes upon leading Hymn-Writers and Important Topics in Hymnology; (5) Various Efforts for the furtherance of Practical Church Music through Lectures and Rehearsals outside the Seminary; (6) The Management of the Hosmer Hall Choral Union, whose chorus of about 180 singers is drawn from the whole city of Hartford, and which, during the winter, held 31 full and 39 partial rehearsals, and gave three public performances, namely, Nov. 10, 1883, appropriate music at the Luther Festival; Jan. 25, 1884, representative German and English cathedral music; and May 7, 1884, Handel's oratorio, "The Messiah." The Choral Union has grown with surprising rapidity in every way, until its management has become almost the largest single item in Mr. Pratt's work. The success thus far attained was finely shown in the rendering of "The Messiah" in Anniversary week. It is safe to say that the noble oratorio is rarely given with more genuine and intelligent sentiment, and even, in many passages, with greater technical perfection, than at this concert. The expressive and impressive powers of good sacred music were abundantly illustrated. The crowded audience was not only delighted, but uplifted by the enthusiastic fervor of the performers.

We take occasion here to note the principal purposes in view in the musical department of the Seminary, when it shall be separated, as it should be, from the elocutionary department. Mr. Pratt proposes (1) to give every student thorough training in the elements of music, so far as they are required in sight-reading and in tune criticism ; (2) to give abundant practice in singing church music of every kind; (3) to lecture upon the management of music as a branch of pastoral care; (4) to lecture upon historical and practical hymnology; (5) to foster intelligent interest in church music in the churches by lectures or other means ; and (6), connected with all these lines of effort, to prosecute the work of the Choral Union in studying and performing sacred music of the most elaborate type. Mr. Pratt appears to have made a successful beginning in the development of all these divisions of this unique department. To give it the position of recognized importance in the Theological curriculum which it so richly deserves, the Board of Trustees, at their annual meeting, elected Mr. Pratt Associate Professor of Ecclesiastical Music and Hymnology.

REPORT OF THE INSTRUCTOR IN THE GYMNASIUM.

The work at the Gymnasium consists of an exercise on the chest-weights by all the students ; of the following-out by each man of the particular exercises prescribed for him by Dr. Sargent of the Harvard University Gymnasium ; and of such further general and particular exercises as the Instructor may be able to suggest.

Regular attendance at the Gymnasium is expected of the students four days during the week. The average attendance during the cold months has been something over 50 per cent. of all the students; largest attendance at any one time, 67 per cent. ; average attendance of the Junior class, 81 per cent.

All the students but *two* have used the Gymnasium to some extent. It is perhaps worthy of notice that all the advanced class, five in number, have been regular attendants.

In general it may be said that the value of the Gymnasium is becoming more apparent every year, and is more and more appreciated by the students. It promotes the *general* good health of the students, by giving a better circulation to the blood, by increasing the appetite and helping the digestion, and, too, promotes *sleep* by drawing the blood away from the head into the muscles exercised.

In particular, the value of the Gymnasium is seen in the deepening and expanding of the *chest*, and in the strengthening of the *side* and *abdominal* muscles, which sustain the voice. To this "particular" aim the Instructor has endeavored to direct special attention.

EDWARD A. CHASE.

REPORT OF THE LIBRARIAN.

To the Board of Trustees of the Theological Institute of Connecticut:

The appended annual report of Mr. Richardson is so full, as to results attained and suggestions to be followed, that I will not travel over the same ground, but ask you to approve and support his measures.

The same generous hand which has hitherto contributed to the increase of the library, has given it another admirable impulse in the past year. The need for modern books is really pressing. A larger and fire-proof building is still a want. And organized assistance for cataloguing and collation is also in the future. All these will doubtless come.

The unprecedented growth of the library; its need of constant supervision; the fact that a thoroughly competent successor has sprung up out of our own institution;—all these considerations lead me to return the office which you have entrusted to me for the last six years. I hereby resign the post of librarian.

I must take this occasion to thank you for your cordial support in all the elementary plans, according to which the library has been modeled. Especially must I thank Mr. Newton Case, whose profound interest and far-sighted enthusiasm have led him to institute such beginnings, which it is in his heart to follow out to still nobler proportions. May God spare his life to see the fruit of his own planting.

From four years of associated work with Mr. Ernest C. Richardson, I regard him as an exceptionally competent librarian, and heartily recommend him as my successor.

Respectfully submitted,

C. D. HARTRANFT.

REPORT OF THE ASSISTANT LIBRARIAN.

To the Board of Trustees of the Theological Institute of Connecticut:

The library of the Theological Institute contained, May 1st, 38,256 bound volumes and about 10,000 pamphlets, exclusive of duplicates. Of these 4,081 volumes and 3,000 pamphlets were added during the past year. The sources of accession were: By purchase, volumes 2,601, pamphlets 2,400; by gift, volumes 349, pamphlets 300; by binding of periodicals, volumes 236; transferred from music-room 59.

Among the more important accessions are a complete set of the "Chronicles and Memorials of Great Britain and Ireland," a collection of 2,400 theological tracts of the 16th, 17th, and 18th centuries, and the Beck collection of "Lutherana." This latter collection, of which only a part has arrived, is, probably, by far the best collection of works on the subject in this country, and the collector implies in the preface of his catalogue that it is surpassed by few even in Germany. That a few numbers had been sold before our offer arrived is to be regretted, but the irreplaceable loss is small. The New York *Nation* devoted a half column editorial to the description of this collection last winter, and hoped that some wealthy American would be found to secure it to this country. The generosity of Mr. Case in securing not only this but many other things, which to let pass for the present would be to lose entirely, adds to the debt of gratitude which not only the friends of the Seminary, but of American scholarship in general, already owe to him.

Work of the Year.

As usual, all work has been done by student help. This usually inefficient and always unsatisfactory help, has been more efficient than it has ever been found to be before, during an eight years' experience. This has been partly from the practice begun three years ago of selecting men from the Junior class and pledging them to a reasonable amount of work during the whole course, partly to the very good material for selection, and partly because the organization has been so subdivided that each man has a definite, limited portion of work for which he is responsible, and which he can learn passably well in the limited time he devotes to it.

In the present crowded and unfinished state of things, however, this is the best method. Whether it will be the best when circumstances admit of a more exact method and a more perfect organization will be a question.

The work done includes the cataloguing of books mentioned in last year's report as uncatalogued, also the entire disposal of the books received this year, except a few of the latest accessions, the completion of the biography catalogue with the exception of the books in Room 3, the recataloguing of the Richter books, a considerable progress made on the cards for a shelf catalogue, improvement in the disposition and cataloguing of bound periodicals, the exchanging of nearly 1,000 duplicates and the arranging of all our pamphlets, which were almost entirely untouched, with the cataloguing of a large portion of them. It is hoped that the next report will show the work in pamphlets finished so that the exact figures can be given as of the books. The above figures are only approximate for pamphlets.

Use of Library.

There has been a marked increase in the use of reference books in the library-room; though the cramped quarters make it very inconvenient for many to study at the same time, it has nevertheless been very much used, and a class of books consulted which would surprise those who are not accustomed to unrestricted access to books. It is due largely to the stress laid by the professors upon the necessity of the verification of facts and of studying from the sources; but the increase of the library makes it possible for them, in a few departments, at least, to refer the students to the books needed for consultation. The result is a considerable use by students of a class of books seldom used in most other seminaries, except by professors; and a consequent training in the use of books which cannot fail to be in a high degree useful. The year shows a visible increase in the use of such books.

There have been, during the year, 101 users who have drawn out books to the number of 1,345, an increase of 21 users and 364 books drawn.

Reading-Room.

This was reorganized last year. A few details have been added or improved. By a readjustment of prices the cost of periodicals has been slightly reduced. The transfer to the reading-room of a number of things not hitherto treated as periodicals, and the few additions, makes the total number taken 203 instead of 177, as reported last year. Of these, at least 190 are "periodicals," in the proper sense.

Library-Room.

This has been increased by the addition of a fourth room outside, and more shelving in the basement. Some additional room has been gained by piling books on the tops of the cases. It is safe to say that the usefulness of the library might be nearly doubled if not cramped for room.

Not one-half of the library can be classified under the present circumstances, although cards are being prepared and arrangements made so that it can be done at once when there is room.

In General.

The gift of the Misses Vermilye of Prof. Vermilye's *MS.* sermons and theological lectures, suggests the desirability of making an effort to get the *MSS.* of other of the Seminary professors. It is to be desired that if any such are known to exist, or any *MSS.* of well-known preachers, their deposit in the Seminary library should be secured if possible.

(2.) It is proposed also to make some effort to increase our pamphlets, by persuading people to place them in this library rather than destroy them. It is hoped that members of the Pastoral Union will coöperate in a matter where with so little trouble and cost, so considerable an advantage is gained to the library.

(3.) A study of nearly 175 theological libraries in the United States and Canada strengthens what was said in the report of last year, that no American theological library begins to fill the place of anything more than a relatively good one.

Prof. Curtiss of Chicago, at the dedication of their new library building, well says that "Next to importance to a good faculty for an institution is a well-equipped library."

It is difficult to see how any institution is to rise above mediocrity, so long as its professors are compelled to a mediocrity of scholarship through lack of tools. It can certainly never be true that we can "get just as good an education in America as in Germany," until our resources for books are greatly increased.

This library holds its place, easily, as relatively one of the best theological libraries, and a very few years may put it well above the line of absolute mediocrity.

There is great reason for thankfulness in the present facilities which it offers, and as it increases in efficiency, there is equal reason to hope for a corresponding increase in usefuluess.

ERNEST C. RICHARDSON,
Assistant Librarian.

REPORT OF THE EXAMINING COMMITTEE.

To the Trustees and Pastoral Union of the Theological Institute of Connecticut:

Of the eight members of the Examining Committee appointed by your respective bodies, five reported for duty.

Forty-six of the fifty-four students named in the Catalogue either appeared before them, or were represented by their papers.

Eight absentees—four from the Junior, three from the Middle, and one from the Advanced class—were accounted for by the Faculty.

The Committee were in attendance upon the Oral Examinations on Monday and Tuesday, during which time the Senior class were examined in their presence by the Professors and by the Committee, in Hebrew, Greek, and Church Polity, as were the Middle Class in Theology and History, and the Junior class in Hebrew.

Papers prepared by all the classes in the written examinations held by each Professor during the preceding week were submitted for the inspection of the committee. Specimens of the work prosecuted by the Advanced class, under assignment of the Professors in whose departments the members severally elected to study, were also placed in our hands. From personal investigation at both of these sources of information the Committee draw their report of the respective departments of instruction, which they beg herewith to submit.

Systematic Theology.

The oral examination of the Middle class revealed a maturity of thought and a grasp of the doctrines highly commendable at this stage of the course. A pleasing independence of one another was manifested. The individuality of each student was marked. While encouraged to dig about the foundations of the accepted theology, they adopted substantially, and with but slight variations, the creed of the Seminary as their own. Their familiarity with the points of current discussion concerning the challenged positions of the historic faith, seems rather to have anchored than swerved them from those positions. They will preach Christ, the only Saviour of lost men. They stated the doctrines of the Atonement and the Trinity clearly and with discrimination. The evident conscientious fidelity of the instructor has been met on the part of the class by honest study and intelligent conclusions, limited always by the word of God. The written examination of the Junior class, embracing the General Introduction and Definitions, the Theistic Arguments, the Evidences of Christianity, and the Inspiration of the Scriptures, disclosed the special care and training bestowed at these fundamental points.

New Testament Exegesis.

The examinations under Prof. Riddle indicate work of the highest excellence. The papers of the Junior and Middle classes, and especially the oral exhibit by the Seniors, were characterized by a thoroughness and fidelity to the principles of interpretation, which were as refreshing as they were reassuring.

With special satisfaction we note the training of the students to manly and independent methods of investigation, and to the habit of forming and defending their own conclusions by intelligent acquaintance with the fundamental facts. This feature of exhaustive investigation, accompanied by strict loyalty to a genuine criticism, based upon original manuscript authority, cannot fail to develop champions of the truth,—workmen needing not to be ashamed.

The enthusiasm of the Professor seems to have stimulated the students to faithful work, not only along the lines pursued in the class-room, but in other directions, so that many of the Seniors have read the entire New Testament critically, while all have thus examined the larger part of it. Foundations for future acquisitions have been laid in well-formed habits and methods which will bear fruit in years to come.

We rejoice to see the invincible, grammatical bulwarks of sound doctrine so thoroughly built up in the minds of the outgoing classes, believing that the real defense of the faith is more and more to be found in the *ipsissima verba* of the original text.

We congratulate the Trustees of this Institute upon the substantial and most efficient work which is constantly being done in this department.

Old Testament Languages and Literature.

Of this department your committee have only good things to report. Written and oral examinations have alike borne testimony to faithful effort and enthusiastic interest on the part of professors and students.

The Junior class were closely examined for an hour and a half on Old Testament Introduction, Hebrew Grammar, and Exegesis, and they sustained themselves in a manner highly creditable to Prof. Bissell, and that gave bright promise of future attainment.

The papers of the Middle class covered a great deal of ground, and showed a high average of attainment and remarkable grasp of the questions under consideration. Especial praise should be given for the thorough manner in which the class have mastered the verbal forms, and for the facility which they have acquired in translation.

We should, of course, look to the entire three years' work of the Senior class in order to learn just what the Seminary is able to do in this department. And we call special attention to the following facts: The Senior class have read eleven whole books and parts of five others in the class-room. Yet, so interested have they become in the language, that seven of the class have pursued their studies in the remaining books. One member has completed the reading of the entire thirty-nine books of the Old Testament; another of thirty-one whole books and parts of three others; a third of thirty-one books and parts of two more; a fourth of twenty-seven whole books and parts of four, and a fifth of sixteen entire books with parts of four others. Moreover, one member of the class has prepared a complete vocabulary of the First Book of Samuel, which, together with the Hebrew text, he has printed under the direction of Prof. Bissell, and with the coöperation of

Professor Brown, of Newton Theological Seminary. The Professors have thus secured a valuable text-book for their own use in their respective institutions which will aid and encourage beginners in the study of the Hebrew. That *thoroughness* has also characterized the studies of this class, appeared further in the satisfactory oral examination which Prof. Thompson conducted with so great vigor and enthusiasm, and which brought out the fact that the class had made solid attainments in all the directions in which Hebrew studies are pursued in our seminaries. The History of Exegesis, and the modern criticism of the Old Testament literature, have also very evidently received careful attention. These facts afford most gratifying evidence that our Seminary is bearing a most creditable part in the very successful efforts of American scholarship to revive the interest in and advance the study of the languages and literature of the Old-Testament Scriptures.

We may well congratulate the Seminary and its friends that Prof. Thompson has been spared to see such results from his life-long efforts in this department, and that his work is being taken up by so able and enthusiastic a teacher as Prof. Bissell.

Practical Theology.

Besides the examination papers in this department, sermons and sermon analyses were submitted to the committee. The theory and practice of sermon preparation seem to have been thoroughly taught and the matter of delivery not neglected. The sermons of the Middle class are evangelical, earnest, practical. In Church Polity the Seniors leave the Seminary with definite ideas of Congregationalism.

We commend both the breadth and thoroughness of this department, and congratulate the Institution that students may here learn the art of preaching and become grounded in a Christian polity which includes Christian doctrine.

Department of Music.

Your committee have gone carefully over the examination papers covering a review of the lectures on Hymnody. We find that the students know hymns, their origin, structure, history, faults, uses and comparative merits.

Since from the character of this department no detailed examination can be given, your committee have sought in other ways to ascertain its worth and efficiency.

We find it more than fulfilling its promise of usefulness and exerting a good influence in the Seminary and for the Seminary.

Historical Theology.

From this department there were submitted: First, papers prepared by the Junior class in the written examination on the "History of Culture." The principles and methods of their study were amply illustrated in their treatment of representative passages from the Old and New Testaments. The archæological allusions of each passage were first of all classified under their respective subjects. Then each specific reference, after being clearly indicated by the Hebrew or Greek word in which it was contained, was fully described or explained. The work in each paper was strictly conformed to the same method and was of very uniform excellence.

Secondly, there were submitted written discussions in Biblical Theology by the Senior class of an aeon of Old Testament History, and of the Second Epistle to the Thessalonians. The papers were marked by the clear apprehension of the province, value, and relations of the historical development of revelation, of the science of which they treated. The discernment and delineation of the way-marks of the great Scriptural truths in the passages under review were most interesting, and the development of the various stages of their progress therein indicated evince a mastery of the principles of this science, whose great and growing importance is so strongly emphasized in this department.

Thirdly, the most conspicuous feature of the instruction in Church History developed by the oral examination was the emphasis laid upon the correct *method* of study. The principal effort seems to be directed more toward indicating the sources, outlay, terminology, relations, and auxiliaries of historical study for the student's independent use, than to the immediate impartation of historical facts and information. The definite characteristics and boundaries of each of the great periods, however, are carefully denoted, and minute study of the more important epochs is required.

To place the student at the fountain-heads of historical knowledge, which is one of the great aims of this department, every member of the class is given a branch of study to work up from its first sources during the year. The value of the *methods* pursued in this department cannot but be of permanent value to the student and can hardly fail to be increasingly appreciated as he grows in years and in ability to use the equipment here provided.

The Advanced Class.

The work required of and accomplished by the Advanced class calls for special mention. While the branches of study pursued by them are optional, *study* is required. Specific work is assigned, supervised, and examined by the Professor in whose department the student elects to pursue an advanced course of study. Four of the class attended the regular exercises of the Junior class in New Testament Exegesis for six months in order to review the application of Textual Criticism, with special reference to questions of harmony. The result was gratifying not only as it appeared in the work of this class, but as seen in the Juniors also, who were so stimulated to special study that a majority of them were prompted to construct for themselves a harmony of the Four Gospels.

Two members of the Advanced class pursued special studies in Exegetical Theology. One devoted himself to the Epistle to the Ephesians, and presented work, in written form, which was highly satisfactory as to method and results. The other collated the text of the Four Gospels from the critical texts and the revised version, adding to his notes on the various reading, a compact " Apparatus Criticus " covering the leading manuscript and other authorities. The results are so exact that it is the design of the Professor to incorporate them in a work soon to be published, which, it is hoped, will prove helpful in the critical study of the Greek Testament.

Three Advanced students read Hebrew, giving special attention to grammatical forms. One of them, also, made a special study of parallel passages in the books of Chronicles and Kings, and prepared a harmony of these passages, thus laying the foundation for valuable critical work in the future.

Two members of this class studied under the direction of the Professor of Systematic Theology. The results of their toil were presented to the Committee in two elaborate and noteworthy monographs, one upon "Evolution and Christianity" and the other on "The Witness of Christ's Assumptions to His Divinity."

To the two students who elected Historical Study there were assigned respectively the periods of Gregory X and Edward VI to work up from the sources. The exhibits given of the mere collation of these sources available in the library, which they made for the development of their subjects, indicated an expenditure of time, toil, and scholarly skill and patience of which "Advanced" students only are capable.

In conclusion, there are two characteristics which all the departments of our institution seem to share.

First. The students are trained to seek the original sources of information on all subjects. They are taught where to find and how to use these sources, and are made conversant also with the history and literature of each department of study. This not only gives them a very noticeable independence of judgment, but, in connection with the large and growing collection of such sources of knowledge in the library, this training in the very processes of authorship, and the cultivation of the scholarly taste and spirit it necessarily involves, promise rich results at no distant day.

The *second* characteristic is that interdependence of the several departments upon each other, which seems to be cultivated by each of them without betraying evidence of the interference of any. To the independence inculcated, this feature of instruction adds the equally-essential elements of intellectual breadth and equipoise, which together go to make the true scholar. Through all, too, there breathes that *spirituality* which marks the men who go hence not only as scholars, but as Christian scholars. It is our belief that their Alma Mater may expect to hear of these sons of hers in the church and the world within the first decade of her second half century.

In behalf of the Examining Committee,
GRAHAM TAYLOR,
Secretary.

ADDRESS TO THE GRADUATING CLASS.

BY PROFESSOR M. B. RIDDLE, D.D.

On behalf of your instructors I am permitted to give some last words of counsel. They will not be new to you, my pupils. Whatever be the field of labor to which each of you may go, and you are to be widely scattered, always and everywhere *be hopeful, be faithful*. Be hopeful, for Christ is Head over all things; be faithful, for He bids it because He deserves it.

I. Sundry theological commotions may seem to be discouraging, but our Master tells us of conflict, and yet asks us to be hopeful. Amid the deplorable tendencies of this age, I find one strong ground for hope. The increased attention paid to exegetical theology, however crude some of its present results may seem, ought to lead the people of God to abundant blessing. Every great revival in the study of God's Word has been followed by an advance in positive theological statement as well as by a revival of religion. For these two are *not* contrary to each other. Indeed, the evil tendencies of the age will, I trust, drive Christian teachers and preachers to the more constant use of the proper weapons in defending the truth. By exegetical and historical methods we must defend what we account the teaching from God; by these methods we believe we can defend it; in these methods we have sought to train you. More than this, your instructors, one and all, believe that the truths emphasized, in our instruction and in our creed alike, are the very truths which give abundant ground of hope in ministerial service. Our task has not been to preserve intact some fossiliferous deposits of theology, but to show you how to find God in His written Word. Yet we make no antithesis between theology and faith; we do not find it necessary " to divide in order to distinguish." We glory in teaching theology, the science above all sciences, as the necessary intellectual basis of that art above all arts, the art of Christian living. Thank God for the testimony, uttered again and again, never more touchingly than in the devotional meeting this morning, that our students do not find their seminary years chilling to their piety. By the same token, we believe that the type of theology taught you here is adapted to make you hopeful in your future labors. We have striven to make God uppermost in your thoughts; to bring you to a heart-recognition of Christ the King as well as the Priest of the New Dispensation; to emphasize your dependence on the Holy Spirit He has purchased and promised. These are the divine facts which make preaching a success. Be hopeful, then, because you do not go on this warfare at your own charges.

Morbid views are often the result of a diseased body. Your physical training here should combine with your doctrinal training to make you cheerful. The happiest men I have ever known were healthy Calvinists. (It is true enough that the men most uncomfortable to themselves and others are often bilious or dyspeptic Calvinists.)

The last book we read together was the Apocalypse. We found in it, not a chronological puzzle, not an armory for pessimists, but a majestic vision of the power and glory of the Lamb that hath been slain. Conflict is abundantly foreshadowed, but the anthem that opens the great vision, that song beyond any Hallelujah chorus of earth, praises our atoning Lord as the Unfolder of God's providence, the Ruler over the centuries, the foreordained Victor in the weary conflict. He that hath overcome to open the book shall overcome on the earth. The Gospel is not set to a minor key. Be strong in that hope which maketh not ashamed, because the love of God hath been shed abroad in our hearts through the Holy Ghost which was given unto us.

II. Be *faithful* as well as hopeful. The two injunctions are inseparable. Gratitude to Christ is the immediate response of a renewed heart, and gratitude to a person naturally takes the form of fidelity. Not as of law, but of grace, are we to fulfill our trust. This motive the Holy Spirit uses, and in the ministry its application is manifold and indispensable. Faithfulness to Christ will guard you against two great mistakes in your aims and methods: first, seeking to please yourself; second, seeking to please others rather than your Master. The two are allied, or rather are polar errors, the result of selfishness.

1. And by pleasing yourself, I mean far more than a life of so-called pleasure. Faithfulness to Christ demands that you leave room for Providence in your plans; that you do not obstinately attempt the impossible, because you are the victim of ideals, cherished more as your own than for Christ's sake. A faithful man will not be forever mourning over the lack of opportunities, or attributing to his surroundings the failures for which he is himself responsible. Learn of your age and circumstances as well as from God's Word what Christ would have you do. Then do your best in that very work. The admonition is given in all business circles, in all places of trust, and it is all the more practical when Christ is the Master to whom we are responsible. It is unfaithful, to be forever scheming to get away from present work, to shirk present duty, because we think our gifts fit us for something else. I am hopeful of you in regard to this; for as a class you have been faithful, diligently attending to your seminary work before everything else. Anything else here is unfaithfulness, as you well know.

We earnestly desire that you keep up your studies; for you it would be blame-worthy to **forget** your Hebrew and Greek, however it may be in the case of those not trained as you have been. But I warn you that scholarship which neglects the immediate duty of your office is only a kind of self-pleasing. Scholarship for its own sake, miserly or pedantic massing of knowledge that yields nothing for Christ's service, or that is uttered only for display, may be as selfish as the sordid heaping up of wealth, or the barbaric splendor of our vulgarest millionaires. For Christ's sake be exact scholars; but sacrifice your noblest ideal of study, if Providence calls you to do some hard work that interferes with it. To do otherwise may seem a noble kind of selfishness, but selfishness it is. When you have learned to submit, to do faithfully, patiently, duty that is most distasteful to you, God may permit you to do the work you like.

2. On the other hand, faithfulness demands that you should seek to please Christ rather than to please others. What does *not* please others is not necessarily pleasing to Christ. The matter is usually one of perspective, or subordination. Yet there will come times when you find direct antagonism between the two. If you do not learn to regard all your duty as primarily due to Christ, you cannot get the sweet habitude of faithfulness. Only this can glorify your whole life. Only with the skill of constant practice in following Christ can you stand firm in the few great emergencies when tempted to go with the multitude against your conscience.

Indeed, faithfulness is true success, though it does not always seem to succeed. As many of you are sons of ministers, you probably know that in our calling also unfaithful men sometimes get the credit belonging to others; schemers after influence carry their ends at the expense of their proper duty; pulpit reputation seems strangely incommensurate with fidelity. These things test our faithfulness, and attest the imperfect sanctification of the Church. But God's verdict is the final one. He succeeds to whom the Master says: "Well done, good and faithful servant."

Yet, my dear pupils, God can say this in this world by His providence. He rules the world, and does make signal demonstration here that faithfulness is success. Often we must wait long to see it, but marked illustrations are usually at hand. We have one here to-night. It is fitting that I should close these remarks, and with them the public utterances of this glad semi-centenary, by pointing to that illustration in unequivocal language. The present dean of the Faculty began his services in the seminary fifty years ago, with a mind capable of great achievements, with scholarly hope and ambitions. At the end of the half century, God be thanked, he is still here with us. But his early ambitions for himself have not been fulfilled. With all his gifts he has been neither author, nor orator, nor ecclesiastical leader. Why? Because faithfulness marked out an apparently humbler path of duty for him. And to-night I can say that I know of few lives so successful; certainly of none more faithful. In a trying and unpopular position, he believed that God had marked out his path for him, and he gave up all that interfered with the nearest duty. Whatever the seminary needed that he could give, he gave; his time, his care, his purse, his instructions in any and every department, his tact, his courtesy, his prayers—for the seminary and its pupils—all for Christ's sake. And with him side by side there stood for many a year, through doubt and trial and overwork, another faithful soul, well known to the older Alumni, strangely taken away before him.

We hope that there is an expanding future of usefulness before this institution; but grow as it may, as the last saying of this glad anniversary as well as the fit enforcement of my counsel to you, my pupils, I may express my conviction that there has been, under God, no more potent factor in its success up to the present hour than the faithfulness of our beloved Prof. Thompson, whose life says to you far better than can any words of mine: Be hopeful, be faithful.

www.ingramcontent.com/pod-product-compliance
Lightning Source LLC
Chambersburg PA
CBHW030351170426
43202CB00010B/1337